THE WRITER'S NOTEBOOK

Craft Essays
from
Tin House

THE
WRITER'S NOTEBOOK

Tin House Books

Published by Tin House Books, Portland, Oregon,
and New York, New York
Distributed to the trade by
Publishers Group West
1700 Fourth St., Berkeley, CA 94710
www.pgw.com

ISBN 13: 978–0-9794198–1-2

First U.S. edition 2009
Interior design by
Elyse Strongin, Neuwirth & Associates, Inc.
Printed in Canada

www.tinhouse.com

CONTENTS

THE WRITER'S NOTEBOOK

INTRODUCTION

LEE MONTGOMERY

To me, writing is purely intuitive, so if I tried to illuminate anything about its craft, I'm afraid it would just result in a lot of arm waving. Thankfully, there are those who write criticism or "teach" writing who are brilliant at distilling and articulating the techniques of the written word. James Wood recently wrote a great book: *How Fiction Works*. E. M. Forster's *Aspects of the Novel* and John Gardner's *The Art of Fiction* continue to be classics decades after their first publications. And personal favorites like *Fiction Writer's Handbook* by Hallie and Whit Burnett, the editors behind early *Story* magazine, can be helpful for those beginning to think about writing.

Still, despite these books, among countless others springing up all the time, many claim writing cannot be taught. The mysterious nature of creativity, the complexities of language, narrative, and form make the "teaching" of writing impossible. It is not brain surgery, as they say. Brain surgery can be taught. A writer's work remains elusive—like alchemy. Nevertheless, those of us who work as writers, editors, teachers, and so forth stoically march forward trying to decipher writing's mysteries for others and ourselves. Over the last ten years, more and more books about how to write have been published. Some may be helpful. Others, which simplify the process into diagrams, plot points, page counts, and scene numbers, are plain silly: writing by number. It is the authority with which these authors (many unknown) distill the process into simple easy steps that is most entertaining. Like miracle diets—"Lose Ten Pounds in Ten Days"—we have the literary equivalent, "Five Steps to Great Characters." It appears the more grandiose the claim and prescriptive the advice, the more hilarious and far-fetched the reality.

During the early days of my life as a writer, I devoured all sorts of how-to books, from the aforementioned classics to the more absurd. The latter were my porno, my bad TV; they offered nothing of any value, really. I forgot everything shortly after I read it. The titles always included some type of promise like *Dare to Be Great, Write to Sell, Write to Break Out,* or *Write to Live.* Even if I could remember anything, I couldn't apply what I had learned. My writing brain lived in a faraway land; I could not find any direct route to this learning. The same thing happened in graduate school. The knowledge gained from reading, reading, reading, talking, talking, talking, and workshop, workshop, workshop sat in one impervious mound of dirt inside my head only to be doled out over time by an invisible (and stingy) hand.

I suppose there are those who find prescriptive advice about writing helpful, writers who can look at a project, identify a structure, use an outline, and get to writing. *One, two, three . . . poof!* But I cannot imagine a world where this is true, a world where one creates great characters in five steps, a world in which one pops books out like laying eggs. In my world, writing is difficult and short cuts are few. The only real way to learn how to do it is to read the work of authors who write well and to, well, write—a lot. Along the way, of course, it is always helpful—and interesting—to talk or listen to writers discuss their process and the work of other writers.

Each summer since 2003, Tin House has been lucky to host writers from all over the country who come to Reed College in Portland, Oregon, to lead workshops and talk about the elements of great writing. By the end of the week, many of us who work at Tin House float around dreamily, humbled and inspired by the talks and readings we witness. Yes, the workshop is for the students, but editors and faculty rarely miss any seminars and panels. Listening to Dorothy Allison talk about place, Steve Almond about sex writing, Chris Offutt about revision, Pete Rock about "show" versus "tell," Susan Bell about Maxwell Perkins's editing of *The Great Gatsby*, and Jim Shepard about using history in fiction is not only fascinating but also essential. Listening to authors of this caliber speak about writing inspires and guides us, leading us to new places, to the work of unknown authors, or back to the work of the old masters.

Such is the spirit in which *The Writer's Notebook* was born.

This little book with its title lifted from the journals of Somerset Maugham is not meant to be comprehensive. The seventeen pieces included here behave more like intimate conversations, like a notebook. Not all the essays were presented at the Tin House workshop. A few originated outside the workshop by writers whose work we admire, some of whom have published with the magazine or books division. Margot Livesey's "Shakespeare for Writers," Jim Krusoe's "Le Mot Incorrect," Antonya Nelson's "Lost in the Woods," Rick Bass's "Keep It Simple," and Kate Bernheimer's and Lucy Corin's looks into alternative literary forms were written especially for this volume or excerpted from past lectures delivered elsewhere.

Also, a CD tucked into the back of this book presents a couple discussions that allow readers to hear from other writers on other topics. "Using Real Life in Fiction and Vice Versa" features a discussion between memoirists and essayists Sallie Tisdale, Anthony Swofford, Chris Offutt, Charles D'Ambrosio, and journalist and novelist Scott Anderson moderated by past *Paris Review* and *Tin House* editor Jeanne McCulloch. The other, "Crafting Character," moderated by author and editor Michelle Wildgen, presents a discussion between Denis Johnson, Ron Carlson, and Dorothy Allison about how characters are born.

We at Tin House are tremendously proud of what we've been able to create with the summer workshop. Still, we agree that great writing cannot be taught, and make no such claim. Rather, we believe that great writing should be celebrated, and we are happy to share these celebrations with you.

PLACE

DOROTHY ALLISON

WHAT DO YOU notice when you first enter a story? Who is talking? Who are they talking to? Where are they standing? What's going on in the background? Is there a background?

There are two primary reasons why people read: boredom, which is my disease, and the need for reliable information, which is my constant motivation. I want to know everything. And I do, indeed, pick up books just to get the information that, in my upbringing, I missed. But I cannot tell you how many stories I pick up, and two people are having a conversation about their sex lives—which is a great place to begin, sex is always a good place to begin—but I don't know who they are, and I don't know where they are. It makes me crazy to step into a story and not know where I am. It makes me crazy when characters are arguing about sex, and I don't know what sex means for them. The story seems to take place in no place.

Most Americans no longer have the history of growing up in a town where their parents grew up and their grandparents grew

up and handed down stories about what came before. We no longer necessarily know the story of *nobody goes down that road
at night because the colonel killed a bunch of people out there
and the ghosts walk the roads.* Used to be that story was told for
generations. No more. If you're American, you've probably moved
at least three times in the last decade. You probably do not live
where you were born. Almost surely, you do not live close to your
parents. Almost surely, you have to invent the place that you are
writing about.

And you're jealous of people you think come from a place that
is generally recognizable—Southerners, who all have porches
and pickup trucks and grandmothers (never mind that bunches
of Southerners come from Atlanta); Bostonians, who can remember that last great blizzard that shut down the city; people
from the Chicago projects; Jews from Staten Island or Queens or
the Lower East Side, who eat pickles and go to the Second Avenue Deli and also have a grandmother. Everybody knows these
places and the people in these places are all assumed to share the
same food and the same language. Their place is a given.

But if you're from a place that no one knows, you have to invent it on the page.

I grew up among truck drivers and waitresses, and, for me,
the place where most stories take place is the place that is no
place for most other people. The truck stop: no place. The diner:
no place. The grocery store: an empty landscape that you do not
ascribe as being a real place. But for me those places are real
places, with a population I recognize and can describe, a people
I love even if they do not always love me.

I can give you detail. I can describe for you the tile they use in most truck stops because truckers have a horrible tendency to puke after having drunk great quantities of beer on top of chili. I know the colors of those tiles. I know, in fact, why 7-Elevens are designed the way they are. I've worked there. I recognize why diners are they way they are—why, in fact, I'll make more money waiting on a booth than on the counter. Those places are real places for me. You probably read my stories to learn more about diners. And waitresses. And truck drivers. And I read to learn about the Jews in Brooklyn, the fishermen of Maine, and the combine drivers in Iowa. I'm lusting after those people I know little about: Bostonians who run along the Charles River in shorts even on snowy gray mornings, South Americans who live halfway up a hillside and speak Portuguese, Amish who somehow wound up in Hawaii and live out near Hilo and grow mangoes and passion fruit. All of these people are profoundly exotic to me, and I ache to know their secrets—especially their secret places.

Place is often something you don't see because you're so familiar with it that you devalue it or dismiss it or ignore it. But in fact it is the information your reader most wants to know.

When I went to college, I would sneak into other people's dorms and look in their rooms. I wasn't out to rob anyone but to learn about who they were and what they had. That, too, is place. All the stuff you've got that you don't see is place—and me, I am your reader, and I want to know all about it. Your reader comes into your narrative to steal knowledge—who you are and what is all around you, what you use, or don't use, what you need, or fear, or want—all that sweet reverberating detail. It is just like me going into those dorm rooms and taking a good solid look around. Your stuff provides telling details from which I can derive all kinds of information about you. I can imagine your self-consciousness, your prejudices, your need to be in control, and maybe even what you are willing to risk or share or not risk or not share. I am making you up in my mind, deriving you from clues you provide, you and your story.

So let's review what place is.

Place is visual detail: manicured grass or scrubby weeds, broken concrete or pristine tarmac glistening with morning dew. Place is conditions: weather, atmosphere. Are the roads crowded or are they empty? When you step outside your house in the morning and you hit that clean, cool sidewalk, are there people walking around? Are they looking at you or are they looking away? Are you lonely? Are you nervous?

Place requires context. Is it responsive? Does it notice me? Or is it porcelain, pristine, and just ignoring my passage through? Are there people on the street who flinch when I smile at them? Is there a reason they do that? Place is where the "I" goes. Place is what that "I" looks at, what it doesn't look at. Is it happy? Is it sad? Is it afraid? Is it curious?

What I am trying to say is that place is not just landscape—a list of flora and fauna and street names. That's not place, that's not even decent research. Which brings me to my other point.

I cannot abide a story told to me by a numb, empty voice that never responds to anything that's happening, that doesn't express some feelings in response to what it sees. Place is not just what your feet are crossing to get to somewhere. Place is feeling, and feeling is something a character expresses. More, it is something the writer puts on the page—articulates with deliberate purpose.

If you keep giving me these eyes that note all the details—if you tell me the lawn is manicured but you don't tell me that it makes your character both deeply happy and slightly anxious—then I'm a little bit frustrated with you. I want a story that'll pull me in. I want a story that makes me drunk. I want a story that feeds me glory. And most of all, I want a story I can trust. I want a story that is happening in a real place, which means a place that has meaning and that evokes emotions in the person who's telling me the story. Place is emotion.

So I'm going to say some unscrupulous, terrible, horrible things that are absolutely true in my mind, if not in yours:

Central Florida is despair.

New York City is sex.

California is smug.

Boston has never gotten over Henry James.

Seattle and Portland lie about their weather.

Iowa City is one hotel room and a chlorine stink away from the suburbs of hell.

I keep a list. I keep track of the places I have been and what I have decided about those places from stories I have experienced or read or heard or dreamed. It's a writer's game, but also a game for anyone who grew up with a sense of not knowing much and trying to figure out what everyone else knows or thinks they know.

NOW I'LL TELL you the place I don't want.

A motel in Iowa City whose windows open onto the swimming pool. Have you been there? Not a Motel 6 or a Days Inn. Probably a Sheraton, maybe the Hyatt, but more likely the Marriott, and definitely not the Four Seasons.

For a year I took a picture of every motel room I stayed in. I lined them up. The only thing different as the year went on was that I was more and more often in rooms with minibars. And you could tell it was a minibar. That was the only difference I could see. The bed is always the bed. There is always a TV; there is always a remote control. Sometimes there are extra pillows. Sometimes there aren't.

It's nowhere. It's no place. And there you are.

If you're lucky, Oprah is on at eleven thirty at night. And you can check out what she's done lately. Try, try, try not to start channel-hopping and watching the ads. You can't afford any of that stuff anyway. It's the middle of the night, three o'clock in the morning, and you're in a room in which the art on the wall is a stylized painting of a flower or an unknown landscape. And I do mean an unknown landscape. Someone is doing these paintings and making money, but it's not an actual artist and that landscape is nowhere you recognize. Also, the mattress is kind of soggy, and you've got one of those covers that you are too hot if you have it on you and too cold if you pull it off. You're awake at three o'clock in the morning and you are nowhere; this is not a place.

Hyatts, Sheratons—that's where all those stories take place in which there is no landscape, in which there is not the mention of a tree or the grass or the weather. There is no weather in a Hyatt. Stories that take place in no place—why would you leave out the thing that will most bring alive what you're trying to do? You think the most important thing is that confident voice of that "I" narrator who, let's be clear, is really you when you were twenty-two, and they didn't treat you right, didn't fuck you right, didn't love you right—Momma, first lover, Daddy, I don't care who it was. But I want the story to burn me. I want the page to crisp my fingers.

You were in that room with him when he said no, he did not want you, and you walked out of the room and it felt as if you were bleeding into your own belly. You went down the stairs, out into the night, and you smelled—what did you smell? Was there the distinct odor of spilled beer on the steps? Were you thinking about how when your daddy left that was all that you could smell on the front steps after he was gone? Is it torn-up weeds that you smell? Somebody was sitting on those steps earlier and she was crying, and she didn't have anything else so she reached down and pulled up the grass and ripped it, and you can smell the torn grass in the air.

Or is it your own skin? You had put on perfume. You had bathed carefully. You had washed your hair. You had used that new soap with lavender scent and flowers. You wanted to be wanted, and no one can ever understand how terrible it felt to be told, no, I don't want you. But you smell your skin, and it stinks of sour disappointment, and *you* don't want you. You can understand why he didn't want to have sex with you. That's place—the smell in the air, the memory, the association. It's all history. You are somebody real who comes from somewhere, and you have been hurt in specific, deep, terrible ways.

Or, it could be that other story.

You have been cared for and loved and made joyful. You expect good things. You expect love. Take a deep breath and what do you smell? Mmmm. You've opened your suitcase and your mother, or your girlfriend, or—oh, my God—your husband of one year who still gets tears in his eyes when you reach for him has tucked something inside. You open up the suitcase and lying there, wrapped in plastic, carefully prepared, is a sugar cookie with anisette. The smell is enough to make your whole body flush with lust. You open it up and breathe it in; you won't eat it now. You think about it. Your mother or your lover or your husband or your best friend sneaked that in there for you to find. You are a person to whom wonderful things happen. And tonight, tonight, when you come back to the Hyatt, more wonderful things will happen. The manager will have left chocolates and a bottle of some perfect complimentary wine, with a glass sitting by it waiting for you, or maybe there will be strawberries dipped in chocolate. You are a person to whom wonderful things happen.

That's place, a place more of us should get to more often.

Place is people.

Place is people with self-consciousness.

Place is people with desire.

My major reason for reading stories is that I get off on knowing other people's secrets. On every level, I get off—I tremble from the power of the sexual charge of the secret and the electrical excitement of suddenly discovering the connections I never made before. I want to know everything and so I need an actual person walking the landscape, responding to it, telling me, in fact, how he or she wound up there. What was the decision-making process? Who is that person in this place? I need to know the person walking the landscape, seeing the landscape, remembering another landscape, putting that landscape on top of this landscape. Then suddenly I'm not in one place, I'm in two places. And there's a narrator, and the narrator is making language choices, and that's a landscape. It's a landscape on the page.

Story is negotiated. Story happens from what we put on the page and what the reader takes off the page. The reader does not always take off the page what we imagine we have put there. Because, as I said, there's a whole bunch of stuff you don't even see anymore. And you don't know who your reader might be. When I read your story, I read it with my imagination and my landscape, my sense of place. I can see the place you tell me only through the filter of the places I can imagine, unless you're really good. And it's not going to be good enough just to tell me that a place is all red brick and that kind of off-white limestone. That's not sufficient. I grew up in Greenville, South Carolina, with clapboard houses. No bricks. What I have is the landscape in which I grew up and the landscapes that I have adapted from every damned book I've ever read, and every damned book I've ever read is in the back of my head while I'm reading yours. Every place every other writer has taken me is in me.

Can you take me somewhere no one else has?

Can you show me a place I don't already have a reference for?

Place is the desire for a door. Place is the desire to get out of where you are. Place is experiencing where you are as a trap. Are you in hell on your way to heaven? Are you momentarily safe in heaven, fearful of falling into hell? Characters that interest me, about whom I am most curious, are always engaged in a journey.

Fear is a wonderful place for writers. A character who is genuinely terrified is in the best place because the reader is going to be terrified as well. The reader is going to be sweaty, anxious, wanting something to happen, turning pages. It's a better place if there are loud noises about which a character is not entirely sure of the cause. Fearful places. The lights have gone out, and the rain's coming down so hard, and loud, she can't hear anything, and it's dark and somebody might be chasing her and she's running and the floor is slippery. The tiles are slippery, they're old and they're worn and she's barefoot and sweaty and sliding, and she thinks she can hear somebody coming behind her. She can hear his boots. She can smell his sweat. He's close enough that she can smell him. He's real. Oh God! He's so damn close! And you know what? You know what?

It's better if the fear is real.

You're sitting at home. You're reading this essay. The lights aren't going to go off; it's not raining. There's nothing to be afraid of. Probably not, anyway. Unless, wait. It's not just anybody running up the hall; it's you—not second-person you, first-person YOU. I'm describing you; I'm in your body. Now, how do I make you know this? How do I make you know you're running up the hall, and you're terrified, and sweat's pouring off you, and you're sliding on the slippery linoleum, and the person behind you with a knife is somebody you have reason to be afraid of?

I'm going to use specific details. I'm going to put you in Portland, Oregon. It's July. It's the last night of a writing conference. Everybody was drinking heavy. The students were all exchanging addresses and phone numbers. And you, you wouldn't give this one guy your phone number. You were feeling really full of yourself because your workshop teacher liked that story you showed her and she said she wanted to read the rest of it and you could send it to her, and you were just feeling so good, and good stuff happens to you, it always does. And you go back to the dorm later than you'd planned, but there's nobody else in the dorm. Listen. It's raining. And the back door slams and there he is. And you didn't give him your phone number, and he's like, "Who the fuck do you think you are?" He's coming up the hall and you're barefoot and you're sweating and you're running and the lights go out and it's raining hard. And just before the lights go out, you see what he has in his hand: he's going to gut you from front to back. Run hard, run fast. It's a specific place. It is your specific tender body that your momma loves so much. That's place.

HARD UP FOR A HARD-ON

STEVE ALMOND

THERE HAS BEEN some discussion about the title. It is not mine. I submitted a number of titles; all were turned down. My first suggestion was "Swing for the Fences with Steve Almond and His Raging, Fictional Man-Bat." I believe that was considered too European. Then I thought, *All right, more on the nose*: "Pussy, Pussy, Pussy, Cock, Cock, Cock, *BLING*." That was maybe too on the nose. The charms of "It's Not Skull-Fucking, Baby—It's Skull-Making-Love" eluded the copy desk. Next it was "You Write a Line, I Got a Pole, Honey," which I thought was great; it called to mind the children's song. Eventually, the money people settled on the "hard-on" thing. What can I tell you? I just work here.

Okay, let's get started with a story called "A Seminal Release." Tragically, I did not write this. It was written by a very sick genius named Nick Flanagan.

Jordan Michael-Thompson was a beautiful girl with an eye for fashion and huge tits that you could grab and squeeze but only if she allowed it. She had an affinity for world music and one day she sashayed hornily into her neighborhood recorded-music store because she was in the mood to buy a compact disc from South Africa. As she walked in she noticed there was a really hot security guard. He had a shaved head and was well over the arena of six feet tall; his eyes were blue and his crotch bulged in a manner that suggested he had a giant dick. She got so much more horny at that point! Jordan winked at the security guard. The security guard returned the wink. "Hello," his hot smile said, reminding her of just what his mouth might be capable of. She got wetter vaginally.

"Can I help you?" he added hungrily, his eyes glued to what he imagined to be perfectionate breasts hidden underneath her six-hundred-dollar cashmere sweater. Had he thought about the treasures that lay inside of her downstairs box, he was sure his wiener might explode within the capri confines of his khaki pants. He tried not to think about that because he was on the job.

Sensually, she took his hand.

"I think you should go on coffee break right now. I need to find a good world music album." She rubbed her fat ones against his uniform as she told him the plan. He was so "sexcited."

"My boss will kill me. I don't even know your name!"

"The only thing you need to know is I don't have AIDS," She said, as she unzipped his pants and fondled his hairy, peach colored ball sack with her smooth, effeminate hands. She leaned in and began darting her healthy pink tongue in and out of his right ear, and his dong began to well up with the juice of man as she did this. He undid her designer belt and slid his worker hands down her pants and into the folds of her thong underwear, careful to note that her sex was as shaved as the top of his head was.

He began to finger wantonly. Her cries rose in volume and she pulled his now hard stick out of the sweaty confines of his pants and underwear. She was happy to note it was the size of a CD tower. And just as fucking hard!!!! He threw her on the floor and began to eat of her. The slobbering wetness within her cooch tumbled into the gaping and welcoming hole of his mouth as he used his powerful tongue to deliver the news. The news was that he was giving her a fantastic orgasm! He turned her on her side and licked her ass afterward. The brownest hole tasted fine to him that day because Jordan was beautiful. She also had something to say.

"Can you recommend any world music to me? Is South Africa good?"

"The racist country?" he replied, positioning his cockmeat within grasp of her pouting lips. "I have the perfect album for you." He got up and his boner looked hot to her as he walked and she licked it and he picked up Paul Simon's album Graceland from the world music shelf, as prejaculate oozed from his swollen urethra. He shoved the CD in her attentive clam, causing her sweat-filled mound to quiver.

"Paul Simon recorded this with South African musicians. I want you to have it." Jordan stumbled out of the building with a compact disc inside her cunt.

It felt like a classic.

So now you're asking yourself: Why is Steve Almond such a sicko? Fair enough. But the reason I wanted to share that story with you is so we can do an exercise. I want you to write the *worst* sex scene possible; the more wantonly, vaginally, pre-ejaculatory, oozingly awful, the better. Part of the reason I encourage you to do this is that it frees you up to write whatever you want to write. The central reason that people muff—I said *muff*—their attempts to write sex is because they are putting pressure on themselves for the scene to be sexy. And any time you feel pressure you start making all the mistakes associated with pressure: the unnecessary similes and metaphors, the needless obfuscation, the genital euphemisms, the fancy words that wind up feeling imposed by the author instead of experienced by the characters.

If you remove the pressure for the sex to be good, it frees you up to write about what really matters, which is the way sex reveals character. That's the central reason to write any scene, especially a sex scene: to lay your characters bare. Of course, that's scary work, which is why writers spend so much time avoiding sex scenes—*the next morning they woke up, there was orange juice, blah, blah, blah*—or, even more frequently, ornamenting them. They find a way to avoid the terrifying truth of what the sexual encounter is going to reveal about the characters.

We all know how awkward and shameful, and ecstatic and wonderful it is to be in a sexual interaction. But most sex writing is nothing like that. So now I want to expose you to some good sex writing.

The following excerpt, which I found in Elizabeth Benedict's *The Joy of Writing Sex*, is from Mary Gordon's wonderful novel *Spending*:

> He put his head between my legs, nuzzling at first. His beard was a little rough on the insides of my thighs. Then with his lips, then his tongue, he struck fire. I had to cry out in astonishment,

in gratitude at being touched in that right place. Somehow, it always makes me grateful when a man finds the right place, maybe because when I was young so many of them kept finding the wrong place, or a series of wrong places, or no place at all. That strange feeling: gratitude and hunger. My hunger was being teased. It also felt like a punishment. I kept thinking of the word "thrum," a cross between a throb and hum. I saw a flame trying to catch; I heard it, there was something I was *after*, something I was trying to achieve, and there was always the danger that I'd miss it, I wouldn't find it, or get hold of it. The terrible moment when you're afraid you won't, you'll lose it, it won't work, you won't work, it is unworkable and you are very, very desperate. At the same time, you want to stay in this place of desperation . . . at the same time, you're saying to yourself, you're almost there, you're almost there, you can't possibly lose it now, keep on, keep on a bit longer, you are nearly there, I know it, don't give up, you cannot lose it. Then suddenly you're there.

How much description is there of the physical act? Barely any, it stops at about line three. So that's Foolish Dogma Number One of writing about sex: *Thou shalt be explicit and tell where all the parts are and where they are going and how the lubrication is progressing and so forth.* Nonsense.

The primary thing that is happening during any sexual interaction between two or more people—or in somebody's head, given that most sex is fantasy sex—is that somebody is thinking. Your thoughts are racing. Gordon shows us that. We move very quickly from a couple of establishing, nonexplicit, details—nuzzling, beard a little rough on inside of thighs—to the real action, which is in the heroine's heart and mind.

And yet, is there any confusion about what's happening physically? No. So how is Gordon conveying the physical reality of what's happening? She is using those great underutilized tools of the trade, syntax and sentence shape, to mirror what's happening to the narrator. Her consciousness is perfectly reflected in those long, galloping sentences as she struggles to get to the place that seems to be eluding her. Gordon uses everything: commas, colons, semicolons—she even uses the dreaded ellipses, something we almost never see—all in an effort to convey the physical and psychic rhythms of the sexual act.

What else is this excerpt about, really, other than sex? Gratitude and hunger, certainly, but there is another word that's pretty striking here: *punishment*. This is primarily an internal dialectic. The narrator is struggling against her capacity to have pleasure, to receive pleasure from this gentleman. It's as if her orgasm is a big test, like the SATs or something. This is a common experience people have, even when they're in the supposed throes of passion. The pressure to "achieve" orgasm. Biologically, as it should happen, most men have somewhat less trouble reaching orgasm. It's less of a narcissistic talisman. For women, it's a much more precarious balance. Gordon is speaking bluntly about what a lot of women experience in a sexual setting. I mean, I don't know a lot of women in that way, but I'm trusting Mary Gordon.

Let's move on to James Salter's novel *A Sport and a Pastime*. If you're wondering if you can write a book that is entirely about sex, the answer is yes. *A Sport and a Pastime* is about an older American, a very lonely ex-pat, who develops an elaborate fantasy life about the sexual encounters of two young people, a younger American ex-pat and his French girlfriend. So bear in mind that this scene is a fantasy:

She is in a good mood. She is very playful. As they enter her building she becomes the secretary. They are going to dictate some letters. Oh, yes? She lives alone, she admits, turning on the stairs. Is that so, the boss says. *Oui*. In the room they undress independently . . .

"Ah," she murmurs.

"What?"

"It's a big *machine à écrire*."

She is so wet by the time he has pillows under her gleaming stomach that he goes right into her in one long, delicious move. They begin slowly. When he is close to coming he pulls his prick out and lets it cool. Then he starts again, guiding it with one hand, feeding it in like line. She begins to roll her hips, to cry out. It's like ministering to a lunatic. Finally he takes it out again. As he waits, tranquil, deliberate, his eyes keep falling on lubricants—her face cream, bottles in the *armoire*. They distract him. Their presence seems frightening, like evidence. They begin once more and this time do not stop until she cries out and he feels himself come in long, trembling runs, the head of his prick touching bone, it seems. They lie exhausted, side by side, as if just having beached a great boat.

"It was the best ever," she says finally. "The best . . . We must type more letters."

It's sort of like I gave Salter the bad sex assignment, isn't it? It's a very different sort of writing than Gordon's, much more explicit. The narrator's vantage point has very little concern for the woman's emotions; she's just evidence of this guy's remarkable sexual prowess. I don't really believe there are masculine and feminine styles of narration—that's a disservice to how complex individuals are—but we can say that this style of narration is clearly expressing, or trying to express, a superannuated masculinity. You'll also notice the language is kind of violent, e.g., the use of a word like prick. It's certainly not sexy, but that word is quite intentional. This lonely narrator constructs the sexual interaction as a fantasy of male power.

What are those lubricants about? Why do the young man's eyes keep falling on them? Here's a hint: *she's on her stomach with her ass in the air.* He keeps looking at these lubricants and they feel like evidence. This is where you have to recall that the scene is an obsessive, even pornographic fantasy, crafted by a lonely older man.

The very idea of anal sex, which is embarrassing to the young guy, might be even more preoccupying for our narrator, who is, after all, imagining a younger man with his big, delicious prick plunging deep inside a woman. Taking this scene out of the context of the novel is unfair, but surely you notice how odd it is for the young guy to feel this sudden squirt of shame. It doesn't quite fit.

So when it comes to writing a sex scene, it's important to keep in mind not only who is doing what but also who is telling the story. In this case, the guy telling the story has a charged relationship to the possibility of anal sex. The revelation of character, in this case, isn't about the two people doing the nasty; it's about the person who needs them to do the nasty.

Okay, let's try something a little bit lighter, a scene that inverses the power dynamic. It's from *Paradise News*, a novel by the very funny British author David Lodge. All you need to know is that the protagonist, Bernard, is a forty-year-old virgin and ex-clergyman. He's never had sex. Yolande is a nurse and a social worker, so she's used to instructing people. They've struck up a relationship and they're now in a hotel room:

Tomorrow there was more light in the room, and they split a half-bottle of white wine from the minibar before they began. Yolande was bolder and far more loquacious. "Today is still touching only, but nowhere is off-limits, we can touch where we like, how we like, OK? And it needn't be just hands, you can also use your mouth and tongue. Would you like to suck my breasts? Go ahead. Is that nice? Good, it's nice for me. Can I suck you? Don't worry, I'll squeeze it hard like this and that'll stop you coming. OK. Relax. Was that nice? Good. Sure I like to do it. Sucking and licking are very primal pleasures. Of course, it's easy to see what pleases a man, but with women it's different, it's all hidden inside and you've got to know your way around, so lick your finger, and I'll give you the tour."

Notice how Yolande carries her educator/caretaker persona right into the act of sex. During intimate situations, people don't drop their essential ways of interacting; in fact, often, those ways become more pronounced. Yolande buzz manages Bernard through the experience.

Also, you'll notice, the passage is almost all dialogue. The author doesn't feel the need to step in and rescue our poor hero. Instead, he allows the rush of events—sweetly imposed by Yolande—to overwhelm Bernard. There is no interceding exposition that allows the reader to step back and take a break. This guy is feeling completely overrun by his circumstances. Notice also how Lodge shows us that Bernard is physically excited, and yet Yolande's tone is entirely matter-of-fact, even clinical. The tension between those two affects is part of the comic effect.

Finally, let's look at a passage from Stephen Elliott's book *My Girlfriend Comes to the City and Beats Me Up*, which is fearless about the role of sexuality in the life of the protagonist. Absolutely fearless. This is from the story "Other Desires":

I make her a cup of coffee. She stands by the window peering cautiously through the blinds to the street. I crawl to her on my knees. She looks down at me skeptically. "You couldn't give me what I want in a million years," she says. She places her leg on a chair and guides my face to her and tells me where to lick and where to suck. "That's where my husband fucks me," she says. I'm stretching my neck as she lifts beneath my chin, surrounded by her legs. "Stop," she says, pushing me away. Stripping her top and skirt. She's getting fat. "Do you think I'm the most beautiful woman?"

"I do," I say. We're going through the motions. The next forty minutes is spent with me trying to please her with my tongue until my mouth is dry and sore.

She slaps me a few times over by the couch and for a moment I think this is going to work. She hits me particularly hard once and I feel my eye starting to swell again and she stops. "Lie down on the bed," she says. "My husband doesn't want me to do this." She slides over me. Of course I'm not wearing protection. Nothing is safe. She rides up over me. Like an oven. She says, "Theo, darling." She grabs my hands and places them on her thighs. She lies on top of me, biting me lightly. I grip her legs and stay quiet. Her chest is against my chest. This is sex. There's no real threat. If I yell loud enough she'll stop, which leaves us with nothing. And when I say I exist only to please her I don't mean it. And when she tells me how beautiful she is it's because she doesn't believe it. Or when she says she has to punish me and asks me if I'm scared, she doesn't mean it. We don't mean it.

Hot.

Okay, maybe not so hot. Maybe the opposite of hot. Like, absolute zero.

This is a very sad passage. It's about when sex doesn't work. Now sometimes the purpose of a good sex scene is to arouse the reader, to serve as an ecstatic affirmation of the character's desire, which should be transmitted to the reader. But there are times when just the opposite is true. The sex shows us how profoundly broken the relationship is. It becomes a powerful way of representing that disconnection.

The most immediate and grueling way Elliott represents this couple's failure is that they can't even bring authentic emotion to their trauma play. They just don't mean it. It's a brilliant passage because we always think, "Well, a good sex scene is predicated on the idea that both characters have so much at risk, and they want it so much." In this case, we know their affair is doomed because the danger is gone, the risk is gone.

I'll leave you with this bit of advice, which comes from my essay "How to Write Sex Scenes: The 12-Step Program." I sort of wish I was kidding, but I'm not. Okay, here's the the money shot:

Step 12: *If you ain't prepared to rock, don't roll*

If you don't feel comfortable writing about sex, then don't. By this, I mean writing about sex as it actually exists, in the real world, as an ecstatic, terrifying, and, above all, deeply emotional process. Real sex is compelling to read about because the participants are so utterly vulnerable. We are all, when the time comes to get naked, terribly excited and frightened and hopeful and doubtful, usually all at the same time. You mustn't abandon your characters in their time of need. You mustn't make of them naked playthings with rubbery parts. You must love them, wholly and without shame, as they go about their human business. Because we've already got a name for sex without emotional content: pornography.

One last piece of advice: read the Song of Songs, which is this absolutely gorgeous, nasty, erotic poem that somehow got smuggled into the Old Testament. It's been teaching the same lesson for five thousand years—that sex should be written like our lives depend on it.

WHEN TO KEEP IT SIMPLE

RICK BASS

As with a life, when a story isn't working as well as it could be—or when it isn't working at all—you've basically got two choices: to endure and accept the failure or to try something different. With the latter choice, fear or even panic can arise, leading the experimenter to overreact. Sometimes grand swinging-for-the-fences yields dramatic and satisfying results, but in my experience an overresponse leads just as many times to an even more dissatisfying result.

A rule I've found helpful in such situations is to try to stay calm and go back to basics, to try to show, in gestures, images, and descriptions as simple as possible, what it is you're trying to convey, and not to try to do it all at once, but break it down into pieces—*when you have to*. Try to say it straight, unless some unspeakable lyricism absolutely compels you, insists, otherwise. Lazy writing—loose word choices—is an obvious and common mistake, but so too is the danger of too many words and, from that, too many thoughts poorly structured. So many of my own basic errors are the result of asking the words to do too much work—or even letting them do too much work, or too much work in the wrong places.

What I mean to say is that the responsibilities of lyricism are immense and dangerous to a text and might sometimes best be avoided, if at all possible—that lyricism implies or makes outright promises that cannot always be delivered. Your ideas can so easily become tangled in your words.

But even before I finish putting down in ink this rule or idea, the *say it straight* rule, I have become tangled already. I don't mean *say it straight* in every sentence, or necessarily even any sentence—only to consider it as a possible exit for the times when you find yourself in editorial trouble. And I don't mean avoid lyricism.

Instead, the rule I want to describe has more to do with simple diction rather than with lyricism. I've found in my own writing that it's one of the simplest rules: when you get too wrapped up in a lofty thought and you can't quite make the ends of a sentence or a paragraph hook back up—when you drop a thread and the burning in your brain is not making it properly onto the paper—such entanglement is not necessarily the result of a fatigued or muddled brain, which is what it feels like, but is instead symptomatic of an overly (for the time being) complex thought. And that's okay. Much as we might be loathe to admit it, there are some thoughts, and some emotions, that are too complicated to be captured or expressed in a single sentence. Your words simply may not be lining up right. The word choices may be tripping up the thought. The thought itself may not be false or unsustainable—you might just need to tighten your diction.

Or not. Maybe the thoughts themselves really are tangled

even if the words are precise and elegant. But try cleaning up the words and diction first—saying it straighter—and if that doesn't work, then begin breaking apart the truths, or purported truths, which are probably shrouded in windiness.

In such instances, what often works best for me after three or four frustrating attempts at unspooling a snarl of multiple and successionary thoughts—each thought spawned by and then staggered upon the rest like some arcane algorithm—is to abandon immediately (if only for the time being) the grandiose swell of ambition or yearning that accompanies such multiplicity of thinking and instead ask myself what in the hell it really is I'm trying to say. What is the one thing, the main thought, the simplest thought?

Say it straight; literally, I'll try to speak the thought out loud, as if in conversation—unaided by the treachery and guile of words on paper and speaking it instead as if in explanation, as when someone asks what it is you're working on, and you use plain language to tell them the synopsis rather than using high-octane dream lyrics.

Lay that much-simpler and less-ambitious sentence down like a tiny placeholder—usually it will involve only the first part of the complex thought—and then proceed anew, liberated, unencumbered by the clot of anxious momentum that earlier led you to that seeming dead end.

Re-tool, comes the frequent comment from editors upon encountering such gridlock. *Re-tool* is in itself such a graceless word—we like to think of our work as being organic, not mechanical. We perceive our work to be slippery with the living and possessing the pulse of respiration rather than the cold interchangeable efficiency of fitted cog and gear—but it remains good and useful advice in a jam.

Ornate sentences and thoughts are harder to sustain and nurture than simple ones. When you get into trouble, prune back, simplify. Hide the complex or ambitious thought, for now, and live to write another day.

Sometimes the problem is not even that the deep thought is all that deep but instead that it is composed of a clustered reiteration, and a packing together, of multiple thoughts that have previously been addressed, so that the gridlocked section—which is usually characterized by making no sense and sometimes is missing a phrase at the end—can be cut entirely. In such good fortune, one feels simultaneously foolish and relieved, hapless and triumphant. An airway is opened back up into the body of the text, the story breathes again.

One of the secondary benefits of this strategy is that, following the heavy excision or simplification, your body and mind will relax. By pruning the ornate, a clarity of focus will be achieved, so that the subsequent sentences that spill from your pen will do so as if from a position of zero-base re-set; your body and mind will seek tenaciously to solve the problem, to prove the answer to the problem through images and sequences canted anew with a slightly different perspective; and from this slight reiteration, those larger and more complex truths, more evasive and fleeting, can be better presented, and maybe even understood.

Often a salmon has to make two or three runs at a falls to get up and over the torrent that surrounds and summons it. I would imagine that sometimes it's all right for the salmon to pause for just a moment to clear its head, to take a breather, before attempting such a fantastic leap a second, and then even a third, time.

This kind of layered or accruing path toward a discovery is

typical of novel writing, but it can also be effective when writing a short story. In stories, with their taut and sometimes compressed pace, there is more than ever an instinctive urge to swing for the fences with big, declarative, snazzy thunderbolt truths.

My own preference (and hence my willingness to spill words like rice at a wedding) is toward the small notes and the disproportionately large amounts of emotion and information they can contain, as well as the utility of their accumulated force, neatly fitted as if into a stone wall that seems simply or even crudely constructed from afar, but potentially dazzling when viewed up close.

On the other hand—and in a living or supple text, there is almost always an other hand—don't be afraid in an early draft to overwrite and to swing for the fences with every sentence, every thought, every emotion. As a writer—not a reader, but a writer—remember that you are granted infinite drafts in which to try to get it right. I suspect there is little harm in initially having pileups of sentences and logic, which are often the result of an accruing eagerness as the writer winds up ever tighter, with reckless enthusiasm, until eventually your reach and grasp exceeds your ability to understand and successfully communicate, and you either end up with two or more truths too large and complicated to be framed within the same sentence, or two truths that end up being oppositional—essentially canceling each other out. No matter, for it is likely that the path that led to that interesting if untenable tangle of riches, while yielding an unsatisfactory destination for the time being, also gave rise to interesting sentences, images, and truths along the way.

Erase, then, the illogical or offensive confused and tangled cluster sentence and proceed. Pick one truth, if two or more get too tangled together to coexist, and travel on.

Nine times out of ten, that second truth will reemerge, if it is a viable one, in its own due time. No one need ever know. Only in the burn pile of your early drafts are you clumsy, unsalvageable, foolish, incapable. This in itself should calm a tangled writer, a confused logistician.

ONE MORE PIECE of advice, or consideration. The great short story writer Barry Hannah is reputed to have given an extraordinarily direct piece of feedback to a writing student who, long ago, disagreed with Hannah's assessment that a story turned in by that writer "wasn't very interesting." (This was back in the days of the "bad Barry," as opposed to the subsequent and current days of the "sweet Barry.")

Reportedly—and the story is so strong that one can only hope it is true, so long as one was not the student involved in the disagreement—the student, still challenging that harsh if frank assessment, demanded, perhaps with less respect than could have been afforded a master craftsman such as Barry, to know how the story could be made more interesting. What—other than having had her parents pay gobs of tuition—could possibly be done that had not already?

The instructor—lost, one can only imagine, in the purer service to art—looked long and hard at the student, as if perhaps trying to assay whether that student could handle the truth, or maybe simply peeved at being addressed disrespectfully, paused a long moment, and then said, "Try making yourself a more interesting person."

34

Who among us, enthralled with the power of the pen in our hand, has not succumbed to this same malady, in which we overlook or forget how easily a reader can and will discard a story, poem, essay, novel?

Horrible, then, might have been Dr. Hannah's candor, but true enough, in so many instances. One of the best things that can happen to a writer is for him or her to feel that he or she is not being heard. One of the worst things that can happen to a writer is for him or her to believe that his or her every utterance will be heard—that there are throngs, in fact, waiting for those next utterances.

In perceiving his or her uniqueness and attempting to speak of it, in any fashion, the writer becomes less unique, more common. I admire the writers who grow and change over the course of a life—a career, if it can and must be called that. Even if the change that comes is sometimes experimental change for change's sake, I think that is good and vital and healthy. Even if the change sometimes leads to failure or a dead end, I think it is useful. I used not to feel that way as a young man, but having seen so many writers repeat themselves—and seeing them lose their readership due to the dulling familiarity of the one-trick pony—I have changed my mind. The successes that occur when a writer changes style are dramatic; the power and elegance of Cormac McCarthy's apocalyptic yet redeeming *The Road*, following not long after the Border Trilogy, or of Annie Proulx's Wyoming Stories, following the long novel *The Shipping News*, come to mind, but even something less than those masterpieces would be a success for more mortal writers. At every stage, there is value in residing as far at the edge of one's comfort zone as is possible.

It takes energy to try different things, after one has for a long time been doing them a certain way—and perhaps worst of all, succeeding at them. It's so easy, instead, to milk the last drops of once-sweet and even the mildest of successes. I would imagine that there are lessons from such writers that apply to the rest of our lives as well, beyond the writing, but for now I am thinking only of the writing.

REVISIONING THE GREAT GATSBY

SUSAN BELL

WE ALL KNOW *The Great Gatsby*. We were forced to read it for high school English. And like most books thrust upon students as another cut in the key that would release them from the prison of formal education, it has an ambiguous luster. We remember we liked it, but we're not sure if our admiration was sincere or derived from a desire to please the teacher—and get out.

An informal survey of my acquaintances suggests that few adults have read *Gatsby* lately. When I reread it in the spring of 2002, at the age of forty-three, I hadn't looked at it in almost thirty years. My early readings of *Gatsby* had been supplanted by images of Robert Redford and Mia Farrow, film having usurped literature, as Fitzgerald himself predicted it would.

I was reminded of this eminent yet largely ignored novel when I read the biography of Max Perkins, by A. Scott Berg. At the time, I was writing a book on the philosophy and practice of editing, and the legendary Perkins was my touchstone. He and Fitzgerald enjoyed one of history's most rewarding editor-writer collaborations. Berg gives a fine account of how Perkins and Fitzgerald, together, refined *The Great Gatsby*. I reread the novel just to see how it matched Berg's account of its making. It floored me. I hadn't expected it to be *that* good. Its every sentence and event feel necessary. Fitzgerald succeeds at the unlikely fusion of ultramodern prose—taut, symbolic, elliptical—and gorgeous lyricism: ornate, fluid descriptions of parties, for example, that rival Tolstoy's descriptions of war. Finally and heroically, Fitzgerald manages to maintain compassion for a humanity he portrays in the most sinister terms.

My interest was editing, though, not just writing, and the author's painstaking edit of *Gatsby* distinguishes it. It is a tour de force of revision. So much so that critics, who rarely mention the edit of a book, commented on the quality of *Gatsby's* rewriting, not just its writing, in reviews. For H. L. Mencken, the novel had "a careful and brilliant finish. . . . There is evidence in every line of hard and intelligent effort. . . . The author wrote, tore up, rewrote, tore up again. There are pages so artfully contrived that one can no more imagine improvising them than one can imagine improvising a fugue." Gilbert Seldes agreed: "*The Great Gatsby* is a brilliant work, and it is also a sound one; it is carefully written, and vivid; it has structure, and it has life. To all the talents, discipline has been added." *Careful, sound, carefully written, hard effort, wrote and rewrote, artfully contrived not improvised, structure, discipline:* all these terms refer, however obliquely, not to the initial act of inspiration, but to editing.

Organization and clarity do not dominate the writing process. At some point, though, a writer must pull coherence from confusion, illuminate what lives in shadow, shade what shines too brightly. *Gatsby* is the cat's meow case study of crossing what Michael Ondaatje calls "that seemingly uncrossable gulf between an early draft of a book . . . and a finished product"—in other words, editing.

In autumn 1924, Fitzgerald sent Perkins the *Gatsby* manuscript. The editor diagnosed its kinks, then wrote a letter of lavish praise and unabashed criticism. "And as for the sheer writing, it is astonishing," wrote Perkins. "The amount of meaning you get into a sentence, the dimensions and intensity of the impression you make a paragraph carry, are most extraordinary." A crucial problem, though, was the hero's palpability. Perkins explained:

> Among a set of characters marvelously palpable and vital—I would know Tom Buchanan if I met him on the street and would avoid him—*Gatsby is somewhat vague*. The reader's eyes can never quite focus upon him, his outlines are dim. Now everything about Gatsby is more or less a mystery i.e. more or less vague, and *this may be somewhat of an artistic intention, but I think it is mistaken*.

Gatsby's vagueness *was* intentional, according to Fitzgerald's December 1 reply: "[Gatsby's] vagueness I can repair by *making more pointed*—this doesn't sound good but wait and see. It'll make him clear." To make Gatsby too clear would make him too human and unheroic. Fitzgerald wanted to clarify Gatsby's vagueness, not Gatsby himself. But in a fascinating turnabout, on December 20 the author wrote again, this time to confess that the vagueness was not altogether intentional:

I myself didn't know what Gatsby looked like or was engaged in & you felt it. If I'd known & kept if from you you'd have been too impressed with my knowledge to protest. This is a complicated idea but I'm sure you'll understand. But I know now—and as a penalty for not having known first, in other words to make sure I'm going to tell more.

Although Gatsby needed to be enigmatic, his mysteriousness had to suggest something precise behind it, and Fitzgerald had to figure out what that was. He needed to do as good actors do: learn his character's whole history to show only a small piece of it.

Fitzgerald used two techniques to discover the full expanse of Gatsby's character: real life models and visual aids. In a letter to Perkins, he wrote:

> . . . after careful searching of the files (of a man's mind here) for the Fuller Magee case & after having had Zelda draw pictures until her fingers ache I know Gatsby better than I know my own child. . . . Gatsby sticks in my heart. I had him for awhile then lost him & now I know I have him again.

Fitzgerald had modeled Gatsby on his neighbor in Great Neck, Edward Fuller. Fuller was involved in various scams, including fraudulent stock dealing. Gatsby, wrote Fitzgerald, "started as one man I knew [Fuller] and then changed into myself." When pressed to develop Gatsby further, Fitzgerald went back to the idea of Fuller and set out to learn more about his model's real-life crimes and attitudes. The old nut goes, "Write what you know," but often a writer is clearer about what he doesn't know and must learn about. One easily gets lost in oneself. The detached concentration that research demands may have helped Gatsby come clear in Fitzgerald's eyes.

Besides research, the writer used visual imagery to flush out his hero. Fitzgerald's wife Zelda's drawings of Gatsby must have made Gatsby more tangible, because after spending time with them the author added several superb physical descriptions. Among them: "His tanned skin was drawn attractively tight on his face and his short hair looked as though it were trimmed every day." This is a good deal better than the original, ultimately (and thankfully) excised description of Gatsby, which is chock-full of generic adjectives and adverbs: "He was undoubtedly one of the handsomest men I had ever seen—the dark blue eyes opening out into lashes of shiny jet were arresting and unforgettable." Finally, after the Perkins critique, the Fuller research, and Zelda's drawings, Fitzgerald came up with this description of Gatsby's smile:

> [Gatsby] smiled understandingly—much more than understandingly. It was one of those rare smiles with a quality of eternal reassurance in it, that you may come across four or five times in life. It faced—or seemed to face—the whole external world for an instant, and then concentrated on you with an irresistible prejudice in your favor. It understood you just as far as you wanted to be understood, believed in you as you would like to believe in yourself, and assured you that it had precisely the impression of you that, at your best, you hoped to convey. Precisely

at that point it vanished—and I was looking at an elegant young roughneck, a year or two over thirty, whose elaborate formality of speech just missed being absurd.

Fitzgerald wasn't satisfied making his hero only more physically palpable. With one smile, he exposes the entire range of Gatsby's character: the sincerity and generosity of the man who flips unpredictably, tragically into blankness and self-absorption. It is safe to say, then, that Jay Gatsby was not written so much as edited into a physical—and metaphysical—presence.

Gatsby was not the only character that needed work. Unprompted by Perkins, Fitzgerald amplified Daisy by stacking a metaphor of paralysis that betrayed her inability to grow up emotionally. In chapter seven, Nick arrives to find Daisy and her friend Jordan lying on a couch in the excruciating summer heat. Referring to the torpor, the women say only, "We can't move." *After* this scene was written, in galley proofs, Fitzgerald returned to chapter one to thread in a prescient phrase that underscores the one above: on seeing Nick for the first time in years, Daisy says, "I'm p-paralyzed with happiness." Daisy's inability to move in chapter seven reverberates with her paralysis from chapter one. The metaphor, begun in the writing, gets built up in the edit.

The Great Gatsby's problems exceeded the need for character definition. In one section, the manuscript, as Perkins put it, "sagged." Fitzgerald had sensed a drag in the prose but couldn't see its cause. Perkins did:

> I think you are right in feeling a certain slight sagging in chapters six and seven . . . I thought you might find ways to *let the*

truth of some of [Gatsby's] claims like "Oxford" and his army career *come out bit by bit in the course of actual narrative.*

In giving deliberately Gatsby's biography when he gives it to the narrator you do depart from the method of the narrative . . . , for otherwise almost everything is told, and beautifully told, in the regular flow of it,—in the succession of events in accompaniment with them.

PERKINS DIPLOMATICALLY COMPLAINED of a common structural flaw: clumping. Fitzgerald had shoved a clump of bio-graphical information into one place. Actors have an expression to describe the mere facts an audience must know to understand the story: they call them *the plumbing.* "I'm not doing the plumbing," some will protest, when asked to say a few lines that explain plot or a character's history but stick out from the action like the proverbial sore thumb. At its best, a book's pipes are laid into the work so suavely that the reader simply feels them func-tion and never notices their cold, hard nature.

But pipes protruded in the original version of the scene in which Nick visits Gatsby after the fatal car accident. The two men go to the terrace and sit "smoking out into the summer night." Into this static setting, Gatsby gushes his life story. "Suddenly he was telling me a lot of things," Nick says. The line is a warning to the reader: be patient, you are about to be hammered with "a lot of" information. Yawn. The historical details of Gatsby's life are given up in a monotonous drone. He explains his Oxford claim, then recounts his teenage reveries, his subsequent apprenticeship with yachtsman Dan Cody, from which followed his army career, during which he met and fell in love with Daisy Fay, after which he received a letter at Oxford telling him he had lost her to Tom Buchanan. Are you with me?

Fitzgerald edited his way out of this clump once Perkins pointed it out to him. He broke up the thick block of data into smaller pieces he judiciously distributed throughout the text and enmeshed in the dialogue and drama. The improvement can be seen in the confrontation between Gatsby and Tom. In the manuscript, this scene carried no reference to Gatsby's Oxford claim or his army career; in the revised proof, Fitzgerald fully explains and seamlessly weaves the Oxford and army stories into the drama. The final version reads:

> Gatsby's foot beat a short, restless tattoo and Tom eyed him suddenly.
>
> "By the way, Mr. Gatsby, I understand you're an Oxford man."
>
> "Not exactly."
>
> "Oh, yes, I understand you went to Oxford."
>
> "Yes—I went there."
>
> A pause. Then Tom's voice incredulous and insulting:
>
> "You must have gone there about the time Biloxi [a poseur who'd falsely claimed he'd gone to Yale] went to New Haven."
>
> Another pause. A waiter knocked and came in with crushed mint and ice, but the silence was unbroken by his "thank you" and the soft closing of the door. This tremendous detail was to be cleared up at last.
>
> "I told you I went there."
>
> "I heard you, but I'd like to know when."

"It was in nineteen-nineteen. I only stayed five months. That's why I can't really call myself an Oxford man."

Tom glanced around to see if we mirrored his unbelief. But we were all looking at Gatsby.

"It was an opportunity they gave to some of the officers after the Armistice," he continued. "We could go to any of the universities in England or France."

I wanted to get up and slap him on the back. I had one of those renewals of complete faith in him that I'd experienced before.

The editor had helped the writer reconceive the information as dramatic.

FITZGERALD OBLIGED HIS editor with no hint of defensiveness or anger. The writer had gone very far on his own with *Gatsby* and was ready for the last editorial push—one he freely admitted he was incapable of envisioning alone. He wrote to Perkins, "Max, it amuses me when praise comes in on the 'structure' of the book—because it was you who fixed up the structure, not me. And don't think I'm not grateful for all that sane and helpful advice about it." In fact, it was Fitzgerald who did the fixing, but the writer needed his editor to point the way and was not embarrassed to say it.

It helped to have an editor as astute and courtly as Perkins and one who knew how to balance general commentary with specific suggestions. It was Perkins who pointed out the importance of the character-defining phrase "old sport," when in a letter he wrote: "Couldn't you add one or two characteristics like the use of that phrase 'old sport'?" Fitzgerald had used the phrase only four times; now he ran with it. In the revised proof, Jay Gatsby says "old sport" incessantly and through it displays an absurd yet endearing self-consciousness. The phrase eventually becomes a spoil of war for Tom and Gatsby:

> "That's a great expression of yours, isn't it?" said Tom sharply.
> "What is?"
> "All this 'old sport' business. Where'd you pick it up?"

And a few pages later, Tom shouts, "Don't you call me 'old sport'!" Fitzgerald, then, edited an ornamental detail so that even as it remained ornamental, it would *matter*. "Old sport" had been a cute effect: now it was Gatsby's weapon, armor, and Achilles' heel in one.

Perkins's influence was more or less limited to the macro-edit. Unlike his editing of Thomas Wolfe's work, Perkins didn't mark up Fitzgerald's text word for word, didn't roll up his shirtsleeves, dig in, and reposition the prose. The micro-edits of *Gatsby* were a solitary endeavor. Fitzgerald was a prose techie who could not merely polish but power up a weak passage, raise the ram of a slow sentence. Take this early one: "The part of his life he told me about began when he was sixteen, when the popular songs of those days began to assume for him a melancholy and romantic beauty." This sentence may seem all right, but I dare any reader to argue its elegance or gravity. Fitzgerald would delete it altogether. In its place, he wrote:

> It was this night that he told me the strange story of his
> youth with Dan Cody—told it to me because "Jay Gatsby" had

broken up like glass against Tom's hard malice, and the long secret extravaganza was played out.

Fitzgerald was driven to edit a sentence silly until it punched. Inclined to clarity when he wrote, Fitzgerald's first forays onto the page were at times—as for most mortal writers—blurred with ambiguity. As Somerset Maugham writes in *The Summing Up*:

> [A cause] of obscurity is that the writer is himself not quite sure of his meaning. He has a vague impression of what he wants to say, but has not . . . exactly formulated it in his mind, and it is natural enough that he should not find a precise expression for a confused idea.

Sure enough, Fitzgerald seems unclear of his meaning in an early draft of the crucial scene at the Plaza Hotel. As Nick listens to Daisy, Tom, and Gatsby bicker, he tells the reader:

> I was thirty. Beside that realization their importunities were dim and far away. Before me stretched the portentous menacing road of a new decade.

A few paragraphs later, as he rides home with Jordan in a taxi, Nick adds:

> I was thirty—a decade of loneliness opened up suddenly before me and what had hovered between us was said at last in the pressure of a hand.

Nick's thoughts are opaque. A threat looms, but he does not say what it is. Fitzgerald is trying to conjure up the narrator, reveal his deepest concerns, but Nick remains hazy. The writer blankets the insufficiency with three multisyllabic words—realization, importunities, portentous—that sound smart and say little.

Now look at the final version of this same passage, after Fitzgerald dramatically reworked it:

> I was thirty. Before me stretched the portentous, menacing road of a new decade.

That's all. He deleted the rest of the paragraph to aim at one point. In the next paragraph, Nick is in the taxi as before, but this time Fitzgerald picks up the line he had held back—the undefined threat—and casts it:

> Thirty—the promise of a decade of loneliness, a thinning list of single men to know, a thinning briefcase of enthusiasm, thinning hair. But there was Jordan beside me, who, unlike Daisy, was too wise ever to carry well-forgotten dreams from age to age. As we passed over the dark bridge her wan face fell lazily against my coat's shoulder and the formidable stroke of thirty died away with the reassuring pressure of her hand.

Fitzgerald took a couple of wordy, imprecise sentences and transformed them into a limpid exposé of a single idea: the loss of youth. The danger of turning thirty is defined: "the promise of a decade of loneliness, a thinning list of single men to know, a thinning briefcase of enthusiasm, thinning hair." The theme of aging underscores the character descriptions and is not a coarse intellectual aside: "But there was Jordan beside me, who, unlike Daisy, was too wise ever to carry well-forgotten dreams from age to age." The final sentence was a detached commentary on a detached relationship; now it is a commitment to human tenderness, however flawed: "the formidable stroke of thirty died away with the reassuring pressure of her hand." By changing "a hand" to "her hand," Fitzgerald created a truer intimacy that offers the poignant conclusion that human affection alone can compensate for the indignities of growing old.

Fitzgerald, Berg writes, "is generally regarded as having been his own best editor, as having had the patience and objectivity to read his words over and over again, eliminating flaws and perfecting his prose." But *The Great Gatsby* would be a different book, and very possibly a lesser one, without Perkins's counsel. Many consider editing as either the correction of punctuation (copyediting) or the overhaul of a book such as Wolfe's *Look Homeward Angel*. The editing of *The Great Gatsby* sits between these extremes—a testimony to a writer's discipline to edit himself and his wisdom to let himself be edited by someone worthy: that is how he crossed the gulf.

CHARACTER MOTIVATION

AIMEE BENDER

TO START I'D LIKE to talk about the idea of expansion versus contraction, of open versus closed. In her book *Mystery and Manners*, Flannery O'Connor, who is my favorite writer who writes about writing, says two plus two should always equal more than four. In other words, you shouldn't be able to boil a story down—the elements of fiction should expand rather than contract. O'Connor fought against the idea that a narrative can be simplified, or made into a theme, or summarized in one line. In *Mystery and Manners*, she asserts that the theme of a story should stretch from the first word to the last and not be something you can separate out and present in one sentence. She talks about this idea in terms of fiction and she also talks about it in terms of religion. A devout Catholic, O'Connor had tired of a falsely devout personality who did not follow what she considered true Christian doctrine. Often, the theme in her stories is redemption and the central action is a moment when a somewhat-despicable person experiences grace. In this way, beneath the story, O'Connor is arguing that religion is not something that can be reduced into a list of things to do; like fiction, it is complex, expansive, and mysterious.

In his interview with Howard W. French, "Seeing a Clash of Social Networks," which was published in the *New York Times* post-9/11, Haruki Murakami discusses closed systems and open systems. He writes that the advantage of a closed system, of fundamentalist thought, is that the answers are clear, you know what's what, and people are happier because if you know that this equals this, then there is less stress. In an open system—and he is equating that with a more democratic society—there are a lot more freedoms, there's more potential for equality, but it's a difficult landscape because you are navigating a field of mystery and trying to figure out what makes sense and what answers are available to you and so there's more stress and less happiness. Murakami isn't making it out as though this world over here is only closed and that world over there is only open—he is saying that at any given moment we operate in closed *and* open systems. It's hard to navigate the open system, but it's also the place where a lot of creativity happens because it's all about questioning. I found that article helpful in navigating worldviews, because Murakami isn't judging; he is neutral in his assessments. He isn't simply saying *the closed system is bad*, but that, actually, in the closed system, people are more content. That seemed shocking and bold to me.

I think that we can approach psychology similarly, that psychology can be both a closed system and an open system or—to use O'Connor's terms—two plus two is more than four. Often, it feels like we've been trained to think of psychology as a one-to-one ratio of motivation to action that isn't fair to the depth of the field. I have many psychologists and psychiatrists in my life. My dad is an analyst; my sister is a psychiatrist. If my friends aren't writers, they're often therapists. This has shaped how I view the world. I like to read books by psychoanalysts: they talk often about creativity; they talk often about things that relate to writing. Ultimately, for me, what's so interesting about psychology are the nuances in the way that humans process experience and the actions that result. We've been trained to believe that psychology is cause and effect, but, actually, our motivations are complicated and messy, and how our actions tie into our motivation isn't always clear.

So how do you work with the idea of motivation in fiction? I've noticed in workshops in which I've participated and in workshops that I've taught, that the idea of character motivation often comes up—*Why did the character do this? Can we find a quick reason?* I'd turn in a story in which a character would be behaving a certain way, and the other students would want to know why. It makes sense that people would have the desire to know why. We all have a psychological acuity that we've learned from our culture, whether or not we are aware of it—the desire to say, "Well, this" and plug it into the story. But the thing I worry about when we tack on a reason is that this approach reduces fiction and it reduces the human mind. It also demeans the character.

I think part of this desire comes from mainstream film, which has a tendency to link an action directly to a reason, to make motivations really clear, and, as a result, the characters are fleshed out too quickly. Some of it also comes from reading books about writing, which often tell you that you should know what your characters want. John Gardner says that in *The Art of Fiction*; Ray Bradbury says that in *Zen and the Art of Writing*; it's a common statement. For many writers, it's probably a very useful comment, but I find it trips me up, because I don't always know what a character wants. I know some things about the character, but to know what he or she wants feels like the final answer, why I'm writing in the first place.

Whenever I try to think about what my characters want —especially in novel writing—it feels very confusing to me. When I was writing my novel, *An Invisible Sign of My Own*, I asked myself, *What does the character want?* And the answer was, *She wants not to want.*

This is all to say that that's okay, to give you permission not really to know what's going on with your characters and to let the writing be a process of discovering that.

Here is something I understand about psychology, and I think it relates to fiction: if you loosen up your understanding of yourself in some way, then who knows how it will affect who you are in the world. In the same way, you can explore an avenue of your character—something about your character's past, or something in your character's present—and you don't know how the reader is going to connect it to what's going on in the story. That gives the reader a wonderful job to do, which is to try to make the links. I don't think you need to plan that in advance, or ever. I think it can happen if you follow what you think is interesting about the character.

In order to do this, you must trust what you don't understand. Our minds are so adept at trying to explain things that you have to shut that instinct down. As a starting point, choose an action that you can't explain. Often, writing about something that you don't fully get—what it's about or what's in it—is actually very useful because it takes you away from talking about theme or talking about abstractions. If you don't know what something is about, you are probably going to be very concrete in your exploration of it. You're going to say, "I don't know what's in this world, so I'm going to be very direct in the way I present it." This gives the reader tons of space to form his or her own interpretations.

In J. D. Salinger's story "De Daumier-Smith's Blue Period," there is a young man whose mother has died. He begins working for an art criticism correspondence course and corresponds with a nun, whom he thinks is a brilliant artist. In one part of the story that I always remember most strongly, he writes to her:

> The happiest day of my life was many years ago when I was seventeen. I was on my way for lunch to meet my mother, who was going out on the street for the first time after a long illness, and I was feeling ecstatically happy when suddenly, as I was coming in to the Avenue Victor Hugo, which is a street in Paris, I bumped into a chap without any nose. I ask you to please consider that factor, in fact I beg you. It is quite pregnant with meaning.

To me, it doesn't matter that he never explains what "that factor" means. Clearly, it is important to the character, but he doesn't say why. It feels great to me that there is something left for me to figure out. It has this shimmer to it. It's Salinger fully trusting what he might not understand; maybe he has a different take on it, but it seems that he feels the image holds its own. The instinct to leave something like that on the page takes a lot of trust.

Another example of this occurs in James Baldwin's story "Sonny's Blues," which is a long, wonderful, rich story. There are two brothers, and by the end of the story, the younger one has had a major epiphany about his relationship with his brother, but it's unclear what exactly was the final straw that made him open up. There are so many parts to the story: they talk about their family, they talk about their relationship during childhood, they talk about their life now, they talk about culture, they talk about society, and then, ultimately, there is a change. But what facilitates that change isn't fully clear. There is no straightforward cause and effect.

In Murakami's short story "The Kidney-Shaped Stone That Moves Every Day," the main character is a writer. In describing the act of writing to a tightrope walker, he says, "What a writer is *supposed* to do is observe and observe and observe again, and put off making judgments to the last possible moment." I think that is a beautiful description of writing; it lets the world be, but also there is a moment, finally, of some kind of opinion. There is that moment, but to hold it off is a lovely and worthwhile goal.

Murakami is not someone you would think of as a psychological writer. He rarely talks about the background of his characters, and he rarely uses flashbacks, but the actions that his characters go through and the landscapes of his books reveal things about the characters through a kind of surrealism. If the character ends up in a strange hotel on a mountain, alone, for weeks and weeks and weeks, and something magical happens, that is actually revealing something about the internal life of the character on its own.

Likewise, Richard Brautigan's story "The Weather in San Francisco" is an example of how to explore character in a surreal way:

THE WEATHER IN SAN FRANCISCO

It was a cloudy afternoon with an Italian butcher selling a pound of meat to a very old woman, but who knows what such an old woman could possibly use a pound of meat for?

She was too old for that much meat. Perhaps she used it for a bee hive and she had five hundred golden bees at home waiting for their meat, their bodies stuffed with honey.

"What kind of meat would you like today?" the butcher said. "We have some good hamburger. It's lean."

"I don't know," she said. "Hamburger is something else."

"Yeah, it's lean. I ground it myself. I put a lot of lean meat in it."

"Hamburger doesn't sound right," she said.

"Yeah," the butcher said. "It's a good day for hamburger. Look outside. It's cloudy. Some of those clouds have rain in them. I'd get the hamburger," he said.

"No," she said. "I don't want any hamburger, and I don't think it's going to rain. I think the sun is going to come out, and it will be a beautiful day, and I want a pound of liver."

The butcher was stunned. He did not like to sell liver to old ladies. There was something about it that made him very nervous. He didn't want to talk to her any more.

He reluctantly sliced a pound of liver off a huge red chunk and wrapped it up in white paper and put it into a brown bag. It was a very unpleasant experience for him.

He took her money, gave her the change, and went back to the poultry section to try and get a hold on his nerves.

By using her bones like the sails of a ship, the old woman

passed outside into the street. She carried the liver as if it were a victory to the bottom of a very steep hill.

She climbed the hill and being very old, it was hard on her. She grew tired and had to stop and rest many times before she reached the top.

At the top of the hill was the old woman's house: a tall San Francisco house with bay windows that reflected a cloudy day.

She opened her purse which was like a small autumn field and near the fallen branches of an old apple tree, she found her keys.

Then she opened the door. It was a dear and trusted friend. She nodded at the door and went into the house and walked down a long hall into a room that was filled with bees.

There were bees everywhere in the room. Bees on the chairs. Bees on the photograph of her dead parents. Bees on the curtains. Bees on the ancient radio that once listened to the 1930s. Bees on her comb and brush.

The bees came to her and gathered about her lovingly while she unwrapped the liver and placed it upon a cloudy silver platter that soon changed into a sunny day.

Brautigan poses a question at the beginning: *who knows what such an old women could possibly use a pound of meat for?* There is an action the character is doing, but it's unclear why she's doing it. The butcher presents an outrageous idea: maybe she's buying the meat for bees. You take that idea as this funny whim of the butcher's. Then the story goes through this very magical progression, which is that the outrageous idea becomes the story itself. So instead of it just being a whim on the part of the butcher, it actually becomes the true thing that is happening in the story. Fiction can do that. The fact that the old woman goes home and the place is full of bees is not something that you would have predicted, it feels totally unexpected, and yet it feels like a wondrous thing that the butcher happened to intuit. All these mysterious and odd behaviors end up having some kind of sense to them. Brautigan places the elements in the story—the old woman, the butcher, the hamburger, and the liver—and each of these elements ends up being very much a part of the story. The story doesn't go somewhere completely different; it stays in this world.

In terms of character, the story is too brief for us to get deeply into the heart of the old woman. But when she opens that door and goes into her home, what does she see? *The Bees are everywhere* . . . Suddenly, her character fills out through the bees, and the bees become the instrument through which we get to know her. As opposed to a clunky descriptive paragraph that would never fit in a piece like this, her background is revealed in a very natural way. We get a sense of her age, and a sense that she still takes care of herself, and a sense that there was another time when she listened to the radio and probably danced. There is a whole world of history that comes in, and the bees are the caretakers of that history. This is not a story that is about character in any traditional way; it's a more intuitive way of exploring character through objects. It's about following hunches about character and really trusting those hunches.

Another tip, going back to what I was saying before, is to remember that things can't be boiled down—allow for mystery. O'Connor writes:

The form of a story gives it meaning which any other form would change. . . .

The result of the proper study of a novel should be a contemplation of the mystery embodied in it. But this is a contemplation of the mystery in the whole work and not of some proposition or paraphrase.

In other words, don't be reductive. Often, writers will rush to an ending that completes, or sums up, or reduces their story as opposed to moving to a place where it goes to something they may not understand and that may be incomplete but is more honest. That rush doesn't do a service to anyone. It doesn't do a service to the work, and it doesn't do a service to the reader. We know that things are complex; we want things to be complex so that, together, we can look deeply into the layers of an open system.

FAIRY TALE IS FORM, FORM IS
FAIRY TALE*

KATE BERNHEIMER

"The fairy tale, which to this day is the first tutor of children because it was once the first tutor of mankind, secretly lives on in the story. The first true storyteller is, and will continue to be, the teller of fairy tales." —WALTER BENJAMIN

"If during a certain period of my career as a writer I was attracted by folktales and fairy tales, this was not the result of loyalty to an ethnic tradition . . . nor the result of nostalgia for things I read as a child . . . It was rather because of my interest in style and structure, in the economy, rhythm, and hard logic with which they are told." —ITALO CALVINO

"Ours is a highly individualized culture, with a great faith in the work of art as a unique one-off, and the artist as an original,

---

*This title is an homage to Jack Zipes's influential study *Fairy Tale as Myth/Myth as Fairy Tale* (Lexington: University Press of Kentucky, 1994).

a godlike and inspired creator of unique one-offs. But fairy tales are not like that, nor are their makers. Who first invented meatballs? In what country? Is there a definitive recipe for potato soup? Think in terms of the domestic arts. 'This is how *I* make potato soup.'" —ANGELA CARTER

OH, HOW I LOVE fairy tales.

With this essay, I'd like to convey what fairy tales mean to me as an artist, which is everything. (Ever since I was a child I have been happiest living in the sphere of a story. That in itself is a fairy tale.)

I'd also like to demystify the idea that fairy tales are of use only to writers of fantasy or fabulism. I'd like to celebrate their lucid form. And I'd like to reveal how specific techniques in fairy tales cross stylistic boundaries. For while the interpretation of fairy tales is a well-traveled path among writers, fairy-tale techniques remain little identified and appreciated.

"The pleasure of fairy tales," writes Swiss scholar Max Lüthi, "resides in their form." I find myself more and more devoted to the pleasure derived from form generally, and from the form of fairy tales specifically, and so I am eager to share what fairy-tale techniques have done for my writing and what they can do for yours. Fairy tales offer a path to rapture—the rapture of form—where the reader or writer finds a blissful and terrible home.

Fairy tale. This term brings to mind a unique form we still recognize and use even after many centuries of manipulation of its discrete techniques. The form survives mutation. It is also adaptable to a diverse range of narrative styles and shapes. Fairy tales magnetize writers who identify themselves as realists, along with surrealists and dadaists and modernists and existentialists and science fictionists and fabulists (not to mention romance novelists and greeting card authors and tabloid headline writers). Yet, in writerly conversations, discussion of their very classical form is often sublimated to an appreciation of their obvious wild and strange moments. That many writers do celebrate the dark, fantastic cosmos of fairy tales is wonderful, but I would also like to see an increased recognition of their artistic dexterity.

You need not even have any conscious interest in fairy tales to appreciate their effect on you. Fairy tales work on all of us; they're so ubiquitous. Writers I speak with are frequently surprised to discover that what they are doing has formal lineage in fairy tales. Sometimes our conversations lead them to incorporate new motifs in their work, or to intensify others, in direct homage to fairy tales. Yet a critical underappreciation of the art of fairy tales sometimes leads to the misinterpretation of these beautifully deliberate gestures as rather unfortunate accidents or diminishments to the verisimilitude of the work at hand. (There are many reasons for this underappreciation, of course, and they are strange reasons and sad. Part of the problem is that many interpretations of fairy tales are burdened with clichés. But that's a topic for a different essay. For now, let's simply say that their association with women and children, with the nursery story, has perhaps played a part. Also, wolf-girls simply alarm.)

So: instead of looking at how fairy tales have been disparaged, let's celebrate their form.

To do this I'd like to focus on four elements of traditional fairy tales: flatness, abstraction, intuitive logic, and normalized magic. I believe that these formal components (though there are others) comprise the *hard logic* of tales that Italo Calvino refers to in one of the epigraphs to this essay. Many authors who love fairy tales refer to this hardness as contributing to their love of the form—but I'd like to go one step further and examine these four components as they relate specifically to the reductive spectrum of mainstream and avant-garde writing. That is, these four technical components from traditional fairy tales may be found to varying degrees in most commonly named styles of writing and therefore an increased understanding of fairy-tale techniques may help resolve the unfortunate schisms that sometimes arise between so-called mainstream and avant-garde writers and critics.[1] (And, despite an emerging affection for fabulism, I think we all know who has the most obvious power in this schism—fairy tales, with their fondness for the underdog, could help disrupt this damaging hierarchy.)

Another premise of this essay is that just as Sylvia Plath's poems (and, actually, she was a poet much interested in fairy tales) have been analyzed far more for their meaning than for their form, so too with fairy tales. I study the interpretation of meaning in fairy tales—there is a pile of scholarly books on my desk in which are buried my worn-out fairy-tale books—and I apply what I've learned to my editing, teaching, and writing in intricate ways. To learn the history of fairy tales is to learn the history of myth, printing, childhood, literacy, violence, loss, psychology, class, illustration, authorship, ecology, gender, and more. My first three novels—scarce of word though they may be (a friend jokes that my novels contain about the same number of words as any chapter in one of her novels)—try to be about all of these, using fairy-tale techniques.

Furthermore, my study of fairy-tale techniques offers a different, very intimate pleasure to me as I work on my novels: the pleasure of language as it shapes story. The tales live inside of me, it seems, and this feels lovely. Fairy tales are the skeletons of story, perhaps. Reading them often provides an uneasy sensation—a gnawing familiarity—that comforting yet supernatural awareness of living inside a story.

Readers of fairy-tale collections, like readers of, well, books, know through these techniques that they are inside of stories, lost or imagined or invented in there.

I assume that nearly everyone remembers a fairy tale from childhood, but just in case, here is one called "The Rosebud" (a German tale as translated by Ralph Manheim) to help get us into the form:

> There was once a poor woman who had two little girls. The youngest was sent to the forest every day to gather wood. Once when she had gone a long way before finding any, a beautiful little child appeared who helped her to pick up the wood and carried it home for her. Then in a twinkling he vanished. The little girl told her mother, but the mother wouldn't believe her. Then one day she brought home a rosebud and told her mother the beautiful child had given it to her and said he would come again when the rosebud opened. The mother put the rosebud in water. One morning the little girl didn't get up out of bed. The mother went and found the child dead, but looking very lovely. The rosebud had opened that same morning.

Of course, we all know the first gesture—"There was once"—
the first thing you always know about a fairy tale is that you are
in it. Immediately it announces that it is a form and that you are
inside the form.

Apart from the fact that I think this is one of the most perfect
stories in the world, it works well to introduce the four fairy-tale
techniques I mentioned earlier. These techniques have shown up
in some way in nearly every literary fairy tale over hundreds
of years from the seventeenth century to the present, across
the globe and across styles. We can find these in a postmodern,
fragmented narrative by Donald Barthelme ("The Glass Mountain"); in a suspenseful, linear narrative by A. S. Byatt ("The
Thing in the Forest"); in a psychological, subversive poem by
Rita Dove ("Beauty and the Beast"); and in a minimal, sentient
poem by Fanny Howe ("Forty Days"). We could name hundreds
of diverse works by hundreds of diverse writers in which we can
easily find basic fairy-tale tropes and techniques.

So let's start with *flatness*. Characters in a fairy tale are always
flat (whether Little Red Riding Hood, Stepmother, Hedgehog, or
Beast.) In "The Rosebud," we have a mother and two children,
one identified only as "the youngest" and one discarded after
the first sentence. Fairy-tale characters are silhouettes, mentioned simply because they are there. They are not given many
emotions—perhaps one, such as happy or sad—and they are not
in psychological conflict. In a traditional fairy tale, a child who
has escaped an incestuous advance does not become a neurotic
grown-up. This absence of depth, this flatness, violates a technical rule writers are often taught in beginning writing classes: that
a character's psychological depth is crucial to a story. In a fairy

tale, however, this flatness functions beautifully; it allows depth of response in the reader. (I have been writing for a few years about how fairy-tale techniques are also prominent in much contemporary visual art. A good example of fairy-tale flatness in visual art is Kara Walker's work. Walker uses enlarged Victorian cutouts, incorporating folkloric imagery into her harrowing and moving narratives of selfhood, gender, and race.)

Flatness, of course, dovetails with the technique of *abstraction*. Fairy tales rely on abstraction for their effect. Not many particular, illustrative details are given. The things in fairy tales are described with open language: Lovely. Dead. Beautiful. In "The Rosebud," there is no explanation of *how* the children are lovely or beautiful. Here we have another very exciting violation: this time of ye olde "show don't tell" rule. Fairy tales tell; they do not often show. I, very naturally as a writer, am inclined toward this absence.

Interestingly, if you look back at traditional fairy tales you will also find a very limited use of color and a heavy reliance on things that are metallic or glass.[2] In many literary versions of "Little Red Riding Hood," you will find the color of her cloak described and the wolf's teeth often are white. Red and white. (See also the German story "Snow-White and Rose-Red" and the slender, gentle use of that tale as a motif in Kathryn Davis's complex contemporary novel *The Walking Tour*.) But there are not many other colors. The wolf is not described as brown; the forest is not described as richly green. The images in a fairy tale are very isolated, very specific. So precise. So deceptively simple.

To cobble the story together, fairy tales use what I call *intuitive logic*, a sort of nonsensical sense. The language of traditional fairy tales tells us that first this happened, and then that happened.

There is never an explanation of why. In fact the question why does not often arise. Things usually happen in a fairy tale when they need to happen, but other things happen that have no relevance apart from the effect of language. *This* is not logically connected to *that*, except by syntax, by narrative proximity. In "The Rosebud," there is no reason to think that the child in the forest has anything to do with the younger girl's death. Likewise the flower opening upon her death. And that elder daughter—what has happened to her? Can you imagine submitting a story to a writing workshop in which the first paragraph introduces two brothers, but one of the brothers is never mentioned again?

In a fairy tale, inside that lyrical disconnect, resides a story that enters and haunts you deeply, I think. You do not doubt that a fairy tale happened just as it was written. This may explain the moniker of fairy tales as "just-so stories" (sometimes used to praise them, sometimes used to disparage them).

In what is considered to be the earliest literary version of "Little Red Riding Hood," called "The Story of Grandmother," the little girl enters the grandmother's hut and a cat on a shelf sees her and says, "You're a slut if you drink the blood of grandmother!"[3] The girl is hardly astonished by the name-calling cat, not to mention its bawdy language, nor is she fazed that the blood of her grandmother might be in play. Like the girl, the reader easily moves to the next sentence, when the little girl approaches the wolf in the grandmother's bed and proceeds to do a striptease. Shocking, perhaps, but when you read the story the poetry is remarkable, and gorgeous.

Despite their reputation as plot-driven narratives, fairy tales are actually extremely associative when you begin to unstitch them. They use intuitive logic.

In "The Rosebud," the older daughter is simply a noun; and yet she exists in the story, has existed in there, for so very long. She is rendered with such syntactic assurance so as to seem fated; the narrative never raises the question of her disappearance. The details in a fairy tale exist in isolation from what is commonly called "plot," yet this has the effect of making everything seem unavoidable, correct. In a way, this is very postmodern—and not unlike what happens syntactically in some poetry that is called "language poetry." Yet the story also feels mimetic, doesn't it? (The stylistic spectrum happily collapses for me—and reveals that wrongly labeled "nonrealism" is one of our oldest forms.)

And of course, this associative quality is also a sort of violation, a violation of the rule that things must make sense. Many fairy tales rely on the sensed relationship of words to story—the art of putting words together in a strange yet marvelous order that simply feels right, no matter how difficult it is to take it apart and try to put it back together again with everyday logic. A fairy tale is a Humpty Dumpty.

The final technique I'll discuss here is *normalized magic*. The natural world in a fairy tale is a magical world. The day to day is collapsed with the wondrous. In a traditional fairy tale there is no need for a portal. Enchantment is not astounding. Magic is normal.

In "The Rosebud," our dear and soon-to-be-dead little girl is not alarmed by the appearance of a child who then vanishes. The mother disbelieves her daughter but is not alarmed. In the fairy tale the magical and the real coexist—this is a technical element. This is craft.

In Lewis Carroll's *Alice's Adventures in Wonderland,* Alice is not worried that a baby she is carrying transforms into a pig: in fact, she simply sets "the little creature down, and felt quite relieved to see it trot away quietly into the wood."[4]

Likewise, in Jean Cocteau's 1946 film *La Belle et La Bête,* Belle is not afraid because the beast is a beast—and not, say, a human—she is afraid because his appearance startles her. It is the shock of his image that scares her, not his nonhuman-ness, that is—not the magic. Lüthi calls this effect "the beauty shock" in fairy tales. Consider how in most versions of "Little Red Riding Hood" the little girl is unafraid that a wolf speaks to her in the woods. Normalized magic. You can call this "suspension of disbelief" if you want, but I prefer the idea that fairy tales require no suspension on the part of the reader; they are already suspended, expanded, enraptured with normalized magic. In fairy tales there is not much ado about fantastic occurrences.

With their flatness, abstraction, intuitive logic, and normalized magic, fairy tales hold a key to the door fiercely locked between so-called realism and nonrealism, convention and experimentalism, psychology and abstraction. A key for those who see these as binaries, that is. Seen through the lens of fairy tales, many works of literature can be understood as literary forms sharing techniques.

Contemporary authors as seemingly texturally disparate as Robert Coover and A. S. Byatt, Haruki Murakami and Stacey Levine, Rikki Ducornet and Alice Hoffman, Ben Marcus and Donna Tartt,

Gregory Maguire and Joy Williams use forms and techniques that have their root in fairy tales—whether consciously on the part of the authors or not—and are on the path of needles and pins in the forest together. In the work of all of these writers one can identify the patterns of flatness, abstraction, intuitive logic, and normalized magic. How each author expands and contracts from that formal template makes him or her an artist. Every writer is like a topsy-turvy doll that on one side is Red Riding Hood and on the other side the Wolf, or on the one side is a Boy and on the other, a Raven and Coffin. The traditional techniques of fairy tales—identifiable, named—are reborn in the different ways we all tell stories.

Perhaps if we recognize the pleasure in form that can be derived from fairy tales, we might be able to move beyond a discussion of who has more of a claim to the "realistic" or the classical in contemporary letters. An increased appreciation of the techniques in fairy tales not only forges a mutual appreciation between writers from so-called mainstream and avant-garde traditions but also, I would argue, connects all of us in the act of living. I am a true believer.

However, a continued underestimation of the techniques of fairy tales and their influence on hundreds of years of writing will lead, instead, to their disappearance. Also, it will lead to some wonderful books being disparaged by some influential critics as difficult or obscure or unreal-seeming. (Here I offer the suggestion that you look back on some books you dismissed on these grounds, if ever you have done such a thing, and consider them again through a fairy-tale lens. Or, if you are writing this sort of book, then take courage here.)

Too often when a fairy-tale motif is recognized in a story or a book, that work is casually referred to as a retelling or an adaptation, in only broad strokes seen as a fairy tale, and sometimes even called "merely a fairy tale." I dislike the hierarchy of "this is more realistic than that, and therefore this is more valuable than that." But many of these so-called nonrealist or fantastic books owe a tremendous amount to classical form—and one of the most classical forms in the world is that of fairy tales.

Finally, and most sadly, along with a dismissal of fairy tales, we sometimes find a dismissal of form.

Emily Dickinson, who also loved fairy tales, knew about form and its importance:

> *After great pain, a formal feeling comes—*
> *The Nerves sit ceremonious, like Tombs—*
> *The stiff Heart questions was it He, that bore,*
> *And Yesterday, or Centuries before?*
>
> *The Feet, mechanical, go round—*
> *Of Ground, or Air, or Ought—*
> *A Wooden way*
> *Regardless grown,*
> *A Quartz contentment, like a stone—*
>
> *This is the Hour of Lead*
> *Remembered, if outlived,*
> *As Freezing persons, recollect the Snow—*
> *First—Chill—then Stupor—then the letting go—*

Hundreds of years, wood, lead, stone, recollection, stupor, letting go. The pattern is topsy turvy in Dickinson's hands, but we recognize the motifs, and she sews them into a shape that shines, sensational and familiar at once.

Fairy tale is form, form is fairy tale.

Long live fairy tales.

Long live form.

NOTES

1. For a discussion of traditional European folkloric formal elements, I point any interested reader to Lüthi's amazing, repetitive, poetic books. His formal studies of European folktales provide a point of embarkation for not only my critical work but also my fiction.

2. A. S. Byatt wrote a wonderful essay about this called "Ice, Snow, Glass" for *Mirror, Mirror on the Wall: Women Writers Explore Their Favorite Fairy Tales* (New York: Anchor/Vintage, 1998), which also appears in her collection *On History and Stories: Selected Essays* (Cambridge: Harvard University Press, 2002).

3. See an excellent translation by Maria Tatar in *The Classic Fairy Tales: A Norton Critical Edition* (New York: W.W. Norton, 1998).

4. And yes, *this* famous fairy-tale novel does employ portals—that is how Carroll makes potato soup. Writers amplify and minimize, hurtle and hoard, those fairy-tale techniques that appeal intuitively to them.

MATERIAL*

LUCY CORIN

SOME BEGINNING WRITERS start off knowing what they want to write about. They have stuff they know that they want other people to know and they have bones to pick. Others just know they want to write. I was one of those. As a beginning writer I kept writing—on scraps of paper or legal pads—in order to feel like I was *making something*. Generally, we are taught to value content over form, to have something to say and then

---

*Consider, as you think about "material," Madonna: the material girl, her material world, the way she made her name not from scratch but from history, how she imagined herself as text and was celebrated for creating and re-creating herself in the world, from the materials of the world. Consider, as well, the placement of this remark in a footnote, how David Foster Wallace (and others before and after him) expanded the place in our consciousness where the material of a footnote can reside, how the physical nature of a prose text is both powerful and malleable, and how its physicality is evident even in the way we name its parts: head, foot, body.

75

"find a form for it" as if one part of what we produce is our stuff and the other is a suitcase we bought to put the stuff in. You find the form to "suit" your content, your material. This is not an unhelpful way to think about things, but it is not the only way. I believe that it is only because I spent so much time working with words *as material* that I have come to have any idea of what I have to say, in words, to and about the world I live in. I learned *from* what I made *what* I was making.

We are also taught, on the sentence level, to make form as invisible as possible, in order that it not "interfere" with content. To do this we must gently/subtly/slyly vary syntax, sentence length, paragraph length so as to distinguish it from an overtly patterned, "less sophisticated," and "visible" text like "See Jane run. See Jane sit. See Jane spit. See Jane split." In order to take readers' minds off patterns of repetition, in order to prevent them from wondering whether this author is a child or an ironic poet, in order to get "back to the story," we should write something like "Jane ran for a while, then rested on a bench, spit, and continued her run." Clearly, this is a story about a jogger named Jane, and, formally, this is a nicely balanced sentence, with its beginning and concluding clauses of similar length and quietly punctuating "spit" for texture. But because it is less "visible" than the four-sentence version—i.e., it looks and reads like more "normal" prose—it keeps the reader's mind focused on the content. In this sort of sentence the form seems to float somewhere behind or below the material, which this sort of writing insists is the information, or the content of the sentences.

Facility with "invisibility" is incredibly important for fiction writers, but clarity and content, as concepts, are a lot more complicated in fiction than they are in, say, a newspaper article or a recipe. Clarity and content in fiction include sound, rhythm, and associative meaning. In some stories, it might actually be very fun, interesting, and moving to read four almost identical sentences in a row. In some stories, we might not even wonder whether or not Jane is jogging. All writing is some combination of visible and invisible forms, and the combination itself is a pattern that is meaningful to me, the rising and falling of my awareness of and attention to one kind of material—content, or what words represent—and another—visible words, ink, like paint, on a page. I believe that all the finest fiction is actively and intelligently engaged in this dynamic.

When you are a student of writing (which of course does not mean you're taking a class; it means you are living, reading, and writing with the intent to become a better and better writer), *you should look at the material you produce to find your material.* This is a handy sentence to have around to say to yourself, because depending on the particular stage of the piece you are working on or the particular moment in your writing life, you should mean one or another thing by each use of the word *material.* Whether you've written a draft that flowed in a smooth or bumpy stream or that accrued painfully or delicately, you have some material to work with and having a *look* at it can help.[1]

THE FOLLOWING DIAGRAMS are of a page from Samuel Beckett's *Molloy* and a page from Ernest Hemingway's "A Clean, Well-Lighted Place." These pages feel very different; they are depicting different sorts of worlds, worlds that have a different relationship with being constructed out of words. Look

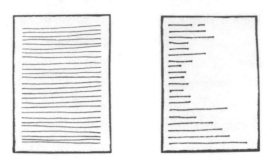

LEFT: Drawing of Beckett's *Molloy*—any page or all pages from the second page until the end of part one, i.e., it's all one paragraph.

RIGHT: Drawing of dialogue from Hemingway's "A Clean, Well-Lighted Place."

how thick and rich (or constipated, depending on your mood) the Beckett page is, how intricate, how dense. Look how airy the page is in the "clean well-lighted place." In your own work, start looking at how your words appear on the page. If you can see a shape, that shape suggests something. You might think of this in terms of character. Can you characterize the physical appearance of a story or a passage? Physical appearance is not a code, but it *is* a significant part of the fictive world you are creating.

And if you can't see a shape, that suggests something, too. It might suggest that you are writing a story that carefully varies the size of its formal units (words, sentences, paragraphs, scenes) without going to extremes such that the prose approximates "invisibility" and seems to be shapeless. It might suggest that you are wobbling all over the place, without attention to the integrity of formal elements, and the result is prose that feels purposeless, that feels "unformed."

BELOW IS A TYPICAL page from J. M. Coetzee's *Waiting for the Barbarians*. The dialogue and the paragraphs are balanced, varied, and integrated, but the scenes are short and visually marked (in this case with asterisks). There's a feeling, reading this book, of falling in and out of a dream, of waking, blinking, and then sliding back under after a breath. But the scenes themselves are soft, elegant realism. Cormac McCarthy's *The Road* is similar in shape—short scenes with breaks—but the size and texture of the sentences and words are less varied than they are in Coetzee's work, and that makes the atmosphere much more stark, the rhythms more overt, more *about* repetition, the sense of day in, day out, in the skeletal landscape in which this novel is set.

When form works, it is indistinguishable from content. Your material is your material.

LEFT: Drawing of a page from Coetzee's *Waiting for the Barbarians*.
RIGHT: Drawing of a page from McCarthy's *The Road*.

IN LYDIA DAVIS'S story "Old Mother and the Grouch," each scene is an argument between the two title characters, and there is literally nothing *between* the arguments—white space

LEFT: A drawing of a typical page or so from Lydia Davis's short story "Old Mother and the Grouch." Again, short scenes of similar size, arranged in a sequence.

RIGHT: A drawing of a typical page from Robert Coover's short story collection *Pricksongs and Descants*, in this case, "The Babysitter." Just by looking at it you can tell that this book is about text, time, and space, a book-length iteration of what a block of text, visual and narrative, means in American culture, how it operates, what it does.

only—not even a sense of which happened when. And that's what this husband-wife relationship is like; it is as if nothing happens to them except one domestic or (significantly) linguistic dispute after another. They argue about Scrabble, for instance, in one scene. Another scene reads, in its entirety:

> A phone call comes from a friend of hers he does not like.
> "It's for you, *angel*," he says, leaving the receiver on the kitchen counter.

The scenes are short, but they are not nearly as geometric as the scenes in the Robert Coover example. Coover's characters are often unstable or morphing caricatures or stylized archetypes—the "ideas" of characters—because that's what he's interested in. His paragraphs, I'm suggesting, look, literally, like the world they depict. Davis's husband and wife, in contrast to their names ("Old Mother" and "the Grouch"), are rendered organically, humbly, specifically, realistically, and the individual, tiny scenes echo this, physically, despite the fact that they are small and in a sequence such that each moment becomes one instance in a series, the narrative perspective circling the characters in their dynamic as it would specimen, snapping pics at all angles.[2] The story is very much about the tension (or, indeed, the "argument") between feeling like a real person and feeling like the idea of a person: an Old Mother, a Grouch. It is a terrible thing to feel like a character, to feel like "the sort of person who . . ." and I think part of the way this story creates this feeling is by existing in a form that creates a specific tension between seeming "real" and seeming "depicted."

WHEN READING, I also think a lot about where, physically, in the story, different kinds of events happen—not only events as in action and depictions of emotion but also events such as ideas blinking through and then coming together, or sound patterns. You probably wrote papers in school about themes in books and to do this you went through the text and highlighted every mention of, say, birds, or a bird, or things that were described as birdlike, birdy, or bird-esque. Of course, the more an idea morphs throughout a text, the more fun, and the less mechanical the exercise of discovering the instances. If you disassembled the pages of the marked book along the wall, then you would see the physical pattern made by your highlighted words and passages.

My favorite example (as long as our example is "bird") is the bird in Flannery O'Connor's "A Good Man Is Hard to Find" in which a very symmetrical family of six (parents and grandmother, boy, girl, and baby) along with a stowaway cat (hidden by the grandmother in a valise) pile into their car for a road trip and end up in a clearing in the woods where, one by one, they are taken into the woods and shot by an escaped convict (The Misfit) and his two minionlike underlings.[3] The story is almost always anthologized in textbooks in the "irony" slot, and indeed one of its beauties is how intricately doubled and redoubled everything is. It's a superb example of a story in which every moment reads multiply and microcosmically, literally and figuratively, the epitome of a "tightly crafted" story.

If you open the twenty-two-page version of the story to pages twelve through thirteen, the word ACCIDENT! (in caps, with an exclamation point, making the word itself stand out as an object in a story that does very little of that sort of thing) appears three times. First, it's on the top left corner, next halfway down the page on the right margin, and finally near the bottom of page thirteen, so that what jumps off the page spread visually is "ACCIDENT! ACCIDENT! ACCIDENT!"—a visual suggestion of tumbling, a sort of flipbook, moving diagonally from upper left to lower right (yes, this is also lucky layout), echoing what is happening in the content, which is that after twelve pages of the family driving along, bickering, stopping for lunch, telling stories, etc., the family/family car/direction of the story has flipped over.[4] We're at the literal and figurative turning point of the story, which happens right before the first time the children scream, "We've had an ACCIDENT!"

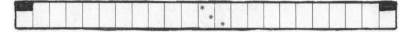

Each box is a page. *= the word ACCIDENT!

NOW I WANT to deepen this idea of form/content unity by highlighting the role of *physicality* (think, in religious terms, of the word made material) in this story.

The grandmother is the protagonist, and the first paragraph of the story establishes this along with her attitude about the trip, as well as the existence of The Misfit, a murderer on the loose. The other thing it does, very quietly, is introduce to us her son, Bailey. He gets two phrases of physical description in this first paragraph: "He was sitting on the edge of his chair at the table . . ." and the grandmother is "rattling the newspaper at his bald head." By the time we get to the middle/turning point of the story, all of the family members have been carefully and equally described concretely: the bratty girl with her curly hair, the bratty boy with his glasses, the prop of a baby, the mother with her broad cabbage face, and, of course, the grandmother dressed in an outfit fit to die in. We haven't seen another physical representation of Bailey, though, in eleven pages. He's been little more than a trembling, glowering, bald guy who says things like "Will you all shut up? Will you all just shut up for one second?" which of course they do not.

So, right before the accident, the cat—leaping out of its bag—"rose with a snarl" and "sprang onto Bailey's shoulder," causing the crash. It is right after the car stops tumbling that Bailey is described concretely again (and now the bird as promised): "He had on a yellow sport shirt with bright blue parrots designed in it and his face was as yellow as the shirt." His physical existence has been withheld from us, in contrast to the other characters,' until this event, when after being bossed around and ineffectual for the first half of the story, he's now got to take some control: the car is upside down, and, a moment later, up walks The Misfit. Poor Bailey. Now that he's finally something more than a baldly poised man on a chair in his own kitchen, he's represented by a ridiculous shirt. The accident itself is framed by these two moments with Bailey (the floundering, bewildered, exasperated driver of this car/story): 1. the cat springing onto Bailey's shoulder and 2. the concrete description of the birds on his shirt.

Next time we *see* him, after everyone has continued not to listen to his fumbled protests for a couple of pages ("Let me handle this!"), he's "squatting in the position of a runner about to sprint forward but he didn't move" (this should remind you, distantly, very deeply under the surface of your consciousness, of page one, where he was seated on the edge—"perched," if you see what I'm getting at . . .) Then, in just a few short paragraphs, "His eyes were as blue and intense as the parrots in his shirt and he remained perfectly still." Bailey and the parrots on his shirt are equally poised for "flight." They are becoming equally alive and not alive. By the end of the page, Bailey has been lead offstage to his doom, with his young son, and meanwhile, the shirtless Misfit is talking about his own father (dead and buried) and his own clothes (which he buried after escaping from prison), and the grandmother (having called after Bailey "come back this instant!") offers The Misfit one of Bailey's extra shirts, and by the end of *that* page, Bailey is dead, at which point the grandmother "could hear the wind move through the tree tops like a long satisfied insuck of breath." We get the movement of invisible air through trees like an invisible bird and life sucked from Bailey in one line, as he becomes a ghost. We spend this page with The Misfit, who continues to talk about his father, whom he might or might not have killed. Then the minions return from the woods, "dragging a yellow shirt with bright blue parrots on it." The Misfit calls for the shirt. "The shirt came flying at him and landed on his shoulder and he put it on. The grandmother couldn't name what the shirt reminded her of."

In the last two pages of the story, it's just The Misfit and the grandmother in the clearing, talking through this morphing web, concluding with the grandmother's great moment of recognition: "You're one of my own children!" (See? Bailey did come back, just as she commanded!) And then *bang*, The Misfit shoots her; she's dead.

So I went though *all that* to show you my diagram of the very specific, isolated pattern of the physical layout of the Bailey-bird-ghost thread of this story, which I contend is *about* physicality (being alive or not, existing or not, being ignored, being recognized/depicted or not, being "in spirit," being dead . . .) in a way that elegantly illustrates my point about form/content unity. Note, too, that while irony, as a device, might begin as a binary, once it is fully "embodied" or dramatized in the story, it is far from a matter of either/or.

Diagram of physical descriptions of Bailey as he transforms into The Misfit via the parrots on his shirt.

1 = "He was sitting on the edge of his chair at the table" and the grandmother is "rattling the newspaper at his bald head."
2 = "the cat . . . sprang onto Bailey's shoulder."
3 = "He had on a yellow sport shirt with bright parrots designed in it and his face was as yellow as the shirt."
4 = "His eyes were as blue and intense as the parrots in his shirt and he remained perfectly still."
* = These two asterisks represent, first, the line about the "insuck of breath" that marks Bailey's death and, second, The Misfit's minion (Bobby Lee) returning from the woods "dragging a yellow shirt with bright blue parrots on it." These two moments manifest Bailey's death in opposite ways: one represented by a specifically nonphysical thing (air moving, life being sucked out); one via a physical thing. So, first the spirit is sucked out, then there's the husk of a body that remains.
5 = "The shirt came flying at [The Misfit] and landed on his shoulder and he put it on. The grandmother couldn't name what the shirt reminded her of."
6 = "'Why you're one of my babies. You're one of my own children!' She reached out and touched him on the shoulder."

The twenty-two pages of the story are represented by boxes, with footnotes to indicate where the *only* concrete physical descriptions of Bailey occur and asterisks to indicate where Bailey's death is manifest in descriptions of other things, creating the transformation of Bailey the grandmother's son into Bailey the symbolic Son in the form of The Misfit.

Now imagine, for instance, that you are drafting this story and you have highlighted all the places where you describe Bailey, but you've also described him some in that space between page one and page eleven. You might start thinking about the content of those descriptions in relation to each other, how they seem to be about this physical transformation from alive to dead, from alive but kind of not existing to what you might call "actually being" a ghost. And that might make you decide to cut some of those lines that interfere with the space in the story where Bailey is not rendered concretely, because you like this way of dramatizing this thing in your story via negative space. This is an example of how having a look at your *material* (words placed variously on paper) can begin to show you what you are trying to say in the story materially (as in content), and here I used an example *about materiality* because that just makes it more fun. I am also one of those writers who has found it to be the case that every piece of writing I love deeply is at some level engaged with physicality/materiality/existence in a way that includes or suggests itself as a work of art.

The story, I like to say and remember, *is always smarter than you*—there will be patterns of theme, image, and idea that are much savvier and more complex than you could have come up with on your own. Find them with your marking pens as they emerge in your drafts. Become a student of your work in progress. Look for what your material is telling you about your material. Every aspect of a story has its own story.

Here are some things to try:
1. Print out your story and put it on a wall. Put it up in a way that allows you to look at it all at once. You might or might not break it up between paragraphs, or scene breaks, or some other obvious structural element that is key to the piece. Look at the patterns of section, chapter, scene, and paragraph size.

Look at how your dialogue is formatted and how it relates to the narrated passages. How buried is one or another element, how lifted from the body of the text to glint in what sort of sun. Try eliminating every "return" in the document, read it like that, and then, without looking at your earlier draft, put in new "returns." See how rhythm steers these choices, the rhythm of reading, and the rhythm of your integration, as a reader, with the text. This creates visible form.

2. Take a highlighter pen and start marking the metaphoric threads, the thematic motifs, the patterns of image, the way sound works or begins to work. Look for what drops off and what accumulates. Ask every aspect you can isolate to have its own story. Ask for a beginning, middle, and end. Ask the holes in the patterns to make the patterns more exciting. Ask for mystery and surprise, which, just as with other sorts of material, does not mean rigid and does not mean sloppy. This creates invisible form.

3. Look at the words and how they are arranged within sentences. Look for capital letters and longness and shortness. Look for the concrete words, look for the abstract words. See if they cluster. Lay some tissue paper over the pages of some books and run a pencil along the lengths of lines, wiggle when you encounter italics, jump when you hit a colon. See what your prose is starting to be, and make it a little more like that. Use what you have before you to guide what you do with it next. Style is form at the sentence level.

I THINK A LOT of writers could benefit from paying more attention to the material aspects of their material, so I've suggested these ways to discover the shapes and patterns—both visible (as in the Lydia Davis example) and invisible (as in the Flannery O'Connor example)—of prose, form, and content. The idea is that then, as you revise, you try to *do* something with those patterns to make them rise or fall into the foreground or the internal workings of a story. Sometimes that means completing them (start with A, go to Z), sometimes it means transforming them (start with A, end with fifty), sometimes that means urging them off center, cracking them, unraveling them, tamping them down, folding them into one another. To make a beautiful piece means you have really witnessed it and really made decisions about it. So, again, material is *content*: he makes a mistake, he makes a bigger mistake, he makes a different kind of mistake, he _____ (learns, doesn't learn, almost learns . . .); the weather comes up three times, it rains, it shines, it blows, and each time it contrasts sharply with the character's mood. And material is also *form*: it's tense; time; point of view; a story told in four linear stretches, each overlapping in time for one paragraph; point of view beginning very close third person, shifting gradually until almost wholly detached/omniscient; it's a series of short clipped lines followed by a long graceful one; or a story told in three parts, five pages/one paragraph/six pages, etc. It's also syllables, consonants, vowels, punctuation, and the white space surrounding everything.

To deal with this, you have to read your drafts in a really dynamic and playfully analytic way, just as you would read a great piece of writing you are trying to learn from. Then you can consider questions like "Oh, the weather came up twice, but not in this last scene—should the pattern be no weather in the last scene, or should the pattern be weather in all the scenes, or should the pattern be weather in all but this one scene in the middle, or every other scene or what?" The answer depends of course on what the choice will make the piece imply, and often you will only discover what that will be by writing it. Sometimes you can anticipate: if you're going to have a pattern of weather in the story, you are suggesting, even "arguing" or "making the case" that there is a relationship between people and events and the "natural" world—and you are characterizing, shaping, creating, demonstrating the qualities of that relationship. So read your work and ask yourself: Is that bullshit or do I believe in what I am suggesting here? Do I believe it because that's what's been suggested repeatedly by the history of the literature I know? Do I believe it because that's what it's like to be alive, right now, or in my memory?

For me, what takes a piece from draft to done is a matter of shifting my sense of my material from what it has meant metaphorically (material as subject matter—that is, words themselves have a metaphorical, indirect, relationship to what they are meant to represent) to what it is literally (material as words, paragraphs, blocks of text; words as words, as opposed to metaphors). In practice, this happens more or less consciously, more consciously the more I'm struggling to make art from mush, and less consciously year by year, the more I write, as the two aspects (working with content, working with form) become more seamless in my own process and more expansive in their possible manifestations.

Thinking visually about language and about story is useful the way all abstractions are useful. Metaphors, for example, seem binary (Bailey's a parrot, the truth is a cat in a bag), or begin that way, just as tensions (a more expansive term for conflict) seem binary. But the more you look at a good one—a good metaphor, a rich tension—the more multifaceted, slippery, and expansive it becomes. Thinking materially about a text, and about the elements that make up a text, is a way of abstracting it so that you can get a sense of a whole that, as a whole, is inconceivable. This is just another way of describing why we write stories, anyway: to have a handle, even for the time it takes to read a story, on a *sense* of the world we live in. So don't think for a second that I am advocating cramming a story into a tidy or phony geometry for its own sake. The same story that lets you see a binary structure can also be a set of nesting bowls, or a blooming dahlia, or a Möbius strip, or a Russian egg, or a zoom-lens telescope, or a deck of cards, or a solar system. Everything moves, so keep that in mind, and ask your stories to keep in mind that whatever they're up to, there's so much more.

NOTES

1. I played around with photocopying, scanning, and shrinking pages from the books I cite in this essay, but I ended up just drawing them. When I was working with the machines, I liked the "truthfulness" of it—if you photocopy and shrink a page of Beckett it really is a black box—but in the end I remembered that I believe in fiction, so I went with the drawings, because I found that I really liked taking the machine-made aspect of a work of fiction (the reproduction of it) and turning it back into something handmade, the way stories themselves are handmade before they are "saved" and reproduced.

2. Why would I suggest that the "organic" is associated with the "realistic" when so much of what we experience in real life is manufactured? As our real-life experiences shift over time, so the text on the page shifts in its associations. Associations within reading culture overlap with lived

experience, but the relationship is complex and all the bodies are in motion. So I believe that what I say about the Davis and Coover stories is true and relevant to both stories, but also entangled and evolving.

3. One might be able to write a craft article without reference to this story, but why? I tried and, honestly, it's not worth the trouble. It may be the case that all lessons about fiction writing are contained within this single document.

4. O'Connor does this sort of thing a lot. "Good Country People," for example, is also divided into two parts that mirror each other thematically as well as structurally.

THERE WILL BE NO STORIES IN HEAVEN

TOM GRIMES

TO ME, WE READ and write stories for a simple reason: we all die. To mitigate our fear of what Nabokov describes as the "criss-cross cause and effect" that governs human existence, we need stories to create the illusion of order. According to Jung's theory of the "collective unconscious," the illogical nature of dreams (and their archetypes) links us to eternity. In dreams, time is absent and causality is meaningless. We can be transformed from an infant lying in a crib into a figure that can fly like a bird without protest. But when we're conscious, time and causality shape our stories; they force upon them beginnings, middles, endings, and, therefore, meaning. Chance may determine our fate, but stories give us closure, which, in turn, prepares us for death. In the finite world of the story, characters have only so long to "live," so for them to move through time meaningfully their *dramatic actions* must have *consequences*, and this directs a story toward closure. For example, Hamlet can kill Claudius only once, and Hamlet can die only once. In heaven, however, Hamlet would be able to die, awaken as if he'd taken a nap, and then kill and die again. There's no story, just repetition. Hamlet's awareness of his finitude prompts his soliloquy and infuses it with melancholy. "To be or not to be" represents a choice between time and timelessness; Hamlet chooses time. He chooses to "suffer the slings and arrows of outrageous fortune" rather than face eternity. He chooses finitude, which gives every story its form.

For writers, our stories are amorphous until we discover how time controls them. Every great story contains a "clock," an intrinsic timekeeper. Lacking this, a story could go on forever. Yet, no matter how great a story is, we long for it to end. Endings offer us solace, and time, not infinity, delivers it. Time organizes, advances, and limits a story, thereby satisfying the reader's craving for narrative coherence and closure.

The Great Gatsby uses time perfectly, and by doing so it makes a small story larger than the sum of its parts. Fitzgerald's "clock" is summer. Notice how quickly his "clock" begins to tick: in the *fourth paragraph* of the novel, its narrator, Nick Carraway, announces that the story ends "[w]hen I came back from the East last autumn." A page later, Fitzgerald rewinds the novel's "clock" as Nick tells us, "The practical thing was to find rooms in the city, but it was a warm season, and I had just left a country of wide lawns and friendly trees, so when a young man at the office suggested that we take a house together in a commuting town, it sounded like a great idea." Two pages later Nick adds, "Across the courtesy bay the white palaces of fashionable East Egg glittered along the water, and the history of the summer really begins on the evening I drove over there to have dinner with the Tom Buchanans." The novel's "clock" is ticking, and we know exactly how long it will continue to do so. But Fitzgerald doesn't simply mention time; he characterizes it. Upon his arrival, Nick visits Daisy and Tom's mansion "on a warm windy evening," at a time of the year when the "lawn started at the beach and ran toward the front door for a quarter of a mile, jumping over sun-dials and brick walks and burning gardens." By page twenty-three we learn that "already it was deep summer on roadhouse roofs and in front of wayside garages, where new red gas-pumps sat out in pools of light, and when I reached my estate at West Egg I ran the car under its shed and sat for a while on an abandoned grass roller in the yard." Gatsby's death signals the end of summer and, shortly afterward, when Nick sees Daisy's husband, Tom Buchanan, it is "one afternoon in late October." Nick leaves West Egg "when the blue smoke of brittle leaves was in the air and the wind blew the wet laundry stiff on the line." Had Nick lived beside Gatsby's mansion for years and repeatedly watched Gatsby gaze at Daisy's "green light," the diffusion of time would have diminished the novel's emotional resonance. Instead, narrative compression generates the novel's power.

By compressing time, you can provide back story with a quality Italo Calvino describes as "quickness." Summing up a character's life swiftly often increases, rather than decreases, a character's depth. Hemingway accomplishes this in *The Sun Also Rises*. Within two sentences, he encapsulates Robert Cohn's life: "He was married five years, had three children, lost most of the fifty thousand dollars his father left him, the balance of the estate having gone to his mother, hardened into a rather unattractive mould under domestic unhappiness with a rich wife; and just when he had made up his mind to leave his wife she left him and went off with a miniature-painter. As he had been thinking for months about leaving his wife and had not done it because it would be too cruel to deprive her of himself, her departure was a very healthful shock." That's "quickness."

In "Reunion," John Cheever encapsulates a father and son's relationship in three pages. The "clock" begins to tick in the story's fourth line: "I would be in New York between trains for an hour and a half." This statement prepares the reader for the story's "quickness," therefore its brevity doesn't feel like a gimmick.

Time also operates like music. Every story has a certain tempo. Cheever's story could be defined as *presto*, meaning "quickly." Despite its relative shortness, Denis Johnson's eight-page story "Car Crash While Hitchhiking" could be defined as *andante*, meaning "at a walking pace." Sentences determine a story's tempo. Let's compare Cheever's to Johnson's.

Cheever's narrator says, "He was a stranger to me—my mother divorced him three years ago and I hadn't been with him since—but as soon as I saw him I felt that he was my father, my flesh and blood, and my future and my doom." Cheever uses dashes, not periods. Also, there's no conjunction between "father" and "flesh."

Johnson's narrator says, "The clouds stayed the same until night. Then, in the dark, I didn't see the storm gathering. The driver of the Volkswagen, a college man, the one who stoked my head with all the hashish, let me out beyond the city limits just as it began to rain." Johnson counterpoints his story's hallucinatory effect with precise grammar. He also uses multiple commas and subordinate clauses to slow its pace.

The tempo of Alice Munro's long stories could be defined as

adagio, meaning "slow and stately." This allows her to layer and complicate her stories so that they feel, at times, like novels. Her story "Carried Away" begins: "In the dining room of the Commercial Hotel, Louisa opened the letter that had arrived that day from overseas. She ate steak and potatoes, her usual meal, and drank a glass of wine. There were a few travellers in the room, and the dentist who ate there every night because he was a widower."

The story begins when Louisa is young and traces her life until she is old. But as the story ends, it loops back to its beginning, making time circular. Also, at the story's climax, when, in a remote town's sawmill, a man's head is accidentally severed at the neck, Munro slows the story's tempo to *grave*, meaning "slow and solemn": "A pile of work clothes soaked in blood lay in the sawdust and Arthur realized that it was the body, the trunk with limbs attached. So much blood had flowed as to make its shape plain at first—to soften it, like a pudding." Munro's dash serves the opposite purpose of Cheever's. His connect for speed. Hers adds a melancholy afterthought to what precedes it, deepening the moment and nearly stopping time.

David Foster Wallace slows time by dividing it into milliseconds in his story "Forever Overhead," which is about a kid leaping from a diving board. The story is nine pages long. Its *objective time* spans no more than a few minutes, but its *subjective time*, which occurs in the boy's consciousness, marks the end of childhood and the beginning of adolescence. The boy sees "girl-women, women, evokers of wows, curved like fruit or instruments, skin burnished brown-bright as staircases of old wonder, suit tops held by delicate knots of fragile colored string against the pull of soft mysterious weights, suit bottoms riding over the gentle juts of hips totally unlike your own, immoderate swells and swivels that melt in light into a surrounding space that cups and accommodates the soft curves as things precious. You almost understand." This subtle emotional change is the story's "clock."

Then there are sprawling novels, Victorian behemoths, modernist labyrinths, postmodern fun houses. By nature, novels require varying tempos. In Tolstoy's *Anna Karenina*, the tempo gallops when Levin is in Moscow and strolls when he's at his dacha in the countryside. In Don DeLillo's *Underworld*, dialogue accelerates the novel's tempo. Here's Nick Shay, the main character, in a pool hall, having a telephone conversation the night before Thanksgiving:

> "Loretta. What are you doing?"
> "Trying on those shoes I bought." . . .
> "That was three days ago."
> "So I'm still trying them on. So what?" . . .
> "So meet me at the car."
> "Meet you at the car? *Now* you want me to meet you?" . . .
> "Tomorrow's off. You don't have to get up for school."
> "I have to get up for the turkey. We have twenty-two people. I'm up at six-thirty. Maybe when they all leave. Tomorrow night."
> "Wear your shoes," he said.

Until the conversation's final line, DeLillo doesn't attribute the dialogue. He also doesn't use adverbs to characterize what's said. The tempo could be defined as *prestissimo*, meaning "as fast as possible." And the conversation is called a "beat": it begins with the shoes and ends with the shoes. Earlier, during the novel's prologue, DeLillo atomizes time by shifting points of view. The "clock" is the length of the baseball game, but DeLillo breaks time down moment by moment, in three one-sentence paragraphs:

"Cox peers out from under his cap and snaps the ball. . . ."

"Look at Mays meanwhile strolling to the plate. . . ."

"Robinson takes the throw and makes a spin move. . . ."

The novel spans the fifty-year Cold War; nonetheless, its "clock" begins to tick when Bobby Thomson hits his World Series–winning home run the same day the Soviet Union detonates its first atomic bomb. The "clock" ceases to tick in cyberspace when a word appears on a computer screen: "Peace."

Conversely, Frank Conroy achieves the opposite effect in his story "Midair." He constructs a "clock" through the use of images. The story begins when the manic-depressive father of "Sean, aged six" dangles the boy out the family's fifth-floor apartment window. Suspended in midair, Sean "stares down at the street, at the cracks in the sidewalk. With the very limited motion available to his arms, he finds his father's belt and hangs on with both fists." Within moments, orderlies from an asylum capture Sean's father and pull the boy into the apartment. The story then describes thirty-six years of Sean's life in brief vignettes, each culminating with an image of Sean suspended in midair. At the story's climax, Sean, now middle-aged, finds himself in an elevator stalled between the sixty-third and sixty-fourth floors of a skyscraper. Beside him stands the elevator's only other passenger, a terrified young man. Sean says to him, "I want you to listen to me, now. We are quite safe." As they wait, Sean "holds the boy's head gently and stares into his eyes." Soon, "the elevator rises, and the doors open. The boy jumps out." He tells Sean to do the same. "Sean smiles. 'This is sixty-four. I'm going to sixty-five.'" The story ends that night as Sean lies in bed, where, "in the darkness, he can see the cracks in the sidewalk from more than forty years ago. He feels no fear—only a sense of astonishment." The "clock" runs out once Sean overcomes his fear of being suspended in midair.

If you're writing your first novel or your first short stories and you are not extraordinarily gifted, you will have difficulty juggling several time lines. This isn't to say that compact, chronological novels can't be funny or moving. Look at *The Catcher in the Rye*: its "clock" is efficient and simply constructed. In the novel's *second paragraph* Holden says, "Where I want to start telling is the day I left Pencey Prep." This is important: Holden makes a direct statement to the reader, which creates the story's "clock" *and* signifies the writer's authority. Don't be coy. The reader *wants* to trust the author immediately. Once a reader's suspension of disbelief is established, the writer's and the reader's imaginations fuse and the story comes alive. *The Catcher in the Rye* is, temporally, a simple novel. Holden is expelled from Pencey Prep and embarks on his trip home. By Christmas, which is only a few days off, Holden's journey *has* to end. Everything of consequence that happens to Holden must happen in those few days. But here's Salinger's brilliant trick: Holden never arrives home. He stops just shy of it. He meets his young sister Phoebe at school and takes her to Central Park, where he tells her to ride the carousel. Soon, it begins to rain. Holden says, "Then what she did—it damn near killed me—she reached in my coat pocket and took out my red hunting hat and put it on my head." Several lines later, Phoebe makes Holden *promise* that he'll go home. "I wasn't lying to her," he admits. "I really did go home afterwards." Yet, soaking wet, Holden remains seated on a park bench, and as he watches Phoebe he confesses that "I was damn near bawling, I felt so happy, if you want to know the truth. I don't know why. It was just that she looked so damn *nice*, the way she kept going around and around, in her blue coat and all. God, I wish you could have been there." With that image, Holden is frozen in time. Salinger's genius was to end his story and yet not end it, to give the reader a sense of closure while leaving the future mysterious and alive. This is why Holden has become, for many readers, eternal. Imagine the maudlin scene of Holden confronting his parents and the ensuing sessions with his "psychoanalyst guy." Salinger adds a coda to Holden's story—a brief summation of events, less than a page long. But the "clock" stops ticking while Holden is seated on the bench.

Here's some final advice: First, determine whether or not your story has a "clock." It can be a day, a week, a month, a season, etcetera, but the story has to have it. Then, to test how well it's keeping time, list the events in your story the way you would list appointments on a calendar. Do not judge them at all, editorially. Just write down what happened and when. If the order is chronologically correct and perhaps contains flashbacks that advance the story, your "clock" is working. Then, note how long each event is:

five lines, five paragraphs, fifty pages. If two people have coffee for fifty pages and then sail around the world in five lines, you have a problem. Fixing the problem won't necessarily be simple, but by understanding that your story needs a "clock" you'll at least know where to start.

THE MERCURIAL WORLDS OF THE MIND

MATTHEA HARVEY

TRYING TO WRITE about imaginary worlds is like breaking a thermometer in a classroom, then trying to collect the little balls of mercury that go shooting off under desks, down the hallway. The slippery silver planets form the most unruly of galaxies. One sneaks into the tread of a student's shoe. One kills a cockroach. Another masquerades as a drop of rain. Yet another subdivides ten times and vaporizes. Mercury, changeable not only in form but also in meaning—planet, metal, messenger to the gods—is an excellent modeling clay for world-making. Mercury the planet, second smallest in our solar system, is nestled closest to the sun, with temperatures that reach 460 degrees Celsius in the day and fall to -180 degrees at night. Like imaginary worlds, it can only be visited by stepping into that shiny rocket with "Imagination" stamped on its sides. Mercury the metal is used not only in thermometers and barometers but in mirrors as well—and so, like an imaginary world, measures and reflects the world we live in. Mercury the messenger, with his winged ankles, travels effortlessly between this world and that, bringing messages to and from the beyond, tracing with those fluttering feet the ties between this world and the ones we invent.[1]

The imaginary worlds I will discuss in this essay are outlandish similes, connected to this world by varying lengths and thicknesses of likeness. And they are connected to each other mostly through their connections to this world. As the spirits tell the heroine of Margaret Cavendish's seventeenth-century novel *The Blazing World*:

> Every humane Creature can create an Immaterial World fully inhabited by immaterial Creatures, and populous of immaterial subjects, such as we are, and all this within the compass of the head or scull; nay not onely so, but he may create a World of what fashion and Government he will, and give the Creatures thereof such motions, figures, forms, colours, perceptions, &c . . . as he thinks best; nay he may make a World full of Veins, Muscles, and Nerves, and all these to move by one jolt or stroke: also he may alter that world as often as he pleases, or change it from a natural world, to an artificial; he may make a world of Ideas, a world of Atomes, a world of Lights, or whatsoever his fancy leads him to.[2]

From Rose Island to Rose Ausländer, or Island Hopping from the Real to the Imaginary

Clearly we need some stable starting point from which to begin, a diving board in this world from which to propel ourselves from the real into the ether, into other realms. Given the potential scope of this inquiry, we'll start small—on a four-hundred-square-foot platform in the Adriatic Sea off the coast of the Italian town of Rimini. On June 24, 1968, this platform declared its independence as a country under the name of "Insulo de la Rozoj," which in its official language of Esperanto means "Rose Island." Rose Island originated as an experiment by an Italian engineer, Giorgio Rosa, who was testing a building technique in which he planted nine pylons in the sea and then attached a platform to them. After that, the story gets a little murky. There are claims (most likely inflated) that the platform housed an illegal radio station, a restaurant, a bar, a nightclub, a souvenir shop, and a post office. It's not clear who the country's "rulers" were—an encyclopedia article mentions that ownership of Rose Island was wrested away from its creator. What is known is that Rose Island asserted its sovereignty by creating its own currency, a set of stamps, and a flag. The Italian government was apparently not very amused by this affair and eventually sent two carabinieri and two inspectors of finance to the island who claimed it for Italy. The government of Rose Island sent a protesting telegram to the Italian government, which the government ignored, and at some later date Rose Island was destroyed by the Italian navy.

Rose Island is an example of a micronation, "an entity intended to replace, resemble, mock or exist on equal footing with recognized independent states."[3] You may not know it—I didn't until spending some time on that ever-expanding world of the Internet—but aside from the boundaries set up by governments—one fixed cookie-cutter shape for England, another for France—there are a number of countries and states that claim to exist, though their borders don't Morse Code their way across any official maps.

It's easy to forget that the countries we live in are inventions. The primordial sludge didn't come with little flags demarcating China here, Chattanooga there. Sludge by definition resists partition.[4] Fast-forward a few hundred centuries, and the world is a quilt of countries and continents that has to be patched and restitched each time the borders shift, or a grapefruit, each section with its capital-city seed. At the same time that the idea of the nation-state was gaining currency in the nineteenth century, the idea of the micronation sprang up too, like the self-portrait's cousin, the caricature, or the earth's attendant moon.

The first micronations included the Cocos (Keeling) Islands in the Indian Ocean and Sarawak, located on the island of Borneo. In both cases, these micronations were under the rule of a family that had bought the land; both were also eventually subsumed (by Australia and Malaysia, respectively). These were micronations that truly wanted to exist as nations. The rulers of Rose Island, on the other hand, seemed less in dialogue with NATO than with Plato. Yet Rose Island was still clearly a product of *this* world, a literal outcropping secured to the ocean floor by its nine pylons. Rose Island was destroyed by its neighbor as if the very existence of the former threatened the reality of the latter. Perhaps the threat *was* real: sitting on this little platform-island at sunset perhaps it was possible to dip your toes into the water of this world and imagine another as the town of Rimini disappeared into the darkness.

In the poem "Progress," Rose Ausländer speaks of life from just such an island. Ausländer (1901–1988) was born in a part of Germany that now belongs to Romania, and so understood the tenuous demarcations of nations. She survived the World War

II Nazi occupation of Bukovina, living in the Jewish ghetto and often hiding in a cellar. On another note, Rose's last name by marriage, Ausländer, literally means "out of the land"—or foreigner. If your last name is Foreigner can you ever be at home?

PROGRESS

I live on the first floor of the first house in the first street of this place. This place is an island. It has only one street. The street has only one house. The house has only one floor. I am the only tenant. I live on fruit and fish. On salty sea air, on sun and rain. On thoughts and dreams. My friends are scattered throughout the world. We write to each other by the bottle-post. I don't know the name of my island. Now and then, a bottle is washed onto the beach. That's how I learn about what's going on in the world, about the great progress being made in all professions. Wars and murders multiply tenfold. Everyone is proud of their war, of their victory, yes, even of their defeat.[5]

The first sentence of this poem sets up a sly progression, locating the speaker in relation to an implied larger world—the first floor conjures up a second and maybe third story, the first house conjures up a second and third house, and the first street multiplies into a grid of streets. However, the poem's second sentence quickly reins in this expansion with the first assertion of boundary: "This place is an island," and the following assertions subtract and subtract until we feel how utterly alone the speaker is. Then the poem moves into its utopic phase, describing the speaker living off the land and her own "thoughts and dreams." Despite the speaker's physical isolation, she is still in intermittent epistolary contact with her friends around the world; in her case putting messages into bottles is the preferred method of communication. It is an ambivalent and inefficient means of communication— after all, the speaker may have a particular person in mind for her message but she cannot control where the waves will take it.[6] These ties to the outside world are tenuous, but information still gets through. When "progress" is mentioned, the tone of the speaker doesn't become apparent until the following sentence: "Wars and murders multiply tenfold." The idiocy and brutality of the outside world is laid bare in the final sentence, "Everyone is proud of their war, of their victory, yes, even of their defeat." Pride blankets every last inch of the earth, except, perhaps, the person living alone on a nameless island. Still, the poem shows that despite an almost micronational isolation, the problems of the surrounding countries cannot be kept out.

A World the Size of a Postage Stamp, or The Power of a Third Lung

I mentioned earlier a certain class of micronations that actually want to be recognized by the world as independent entities. Their attempts to gain legitimacy take the form of reproducing its conventions: becoming a country means minting money, designing a flag, and issuing a set of stamps, thereby enabling the exchange of goods and services, allowing the tugboat instant recognition because of the distinctive piece of cloth attached to its hull flapping against the sky, and, lastly, letting letters be sent from here to there.

Though imaginary worlds do not seek to be recognized as sovereign worlds, the tethers to the real world remain. It's a minimal distinction—if Swift's Lilliputians had sent a telegram declaration of independence it probably would have been too tiny for any queen or president to read, mistaken for a piece of lint, and brushed off the desk. Most writers and inventors of imaginary worlds are probably wise not to ask for official recognition of their worlds given that the result would probably be an FBI file or a trip to a mental-health professional. The worlds' ties to the worlds of their inventors are there, like the string you can only see by tracing the trajectory of the kite down to the outstretched hand. Imaginary worlds always refer back to this world—whether they veil or unveil it, bisect or circle. They can't help but comment.

The Winnipeg-based artist group the Royal Art Lodge sketched a "New Earth," featuring such inventions and revisions as "Catland," a miniaturized "Little U.S.A," "Slime Province," and "Heaven," each an island on a truncated three-quarter globe. It's a revision that only makes sense to someone who has a mental image of the original. Similarly, the stamps issued by micronations are an explicit delineation of the ties between this world and the invented one, adhering here to there with a lick of the tongue. Sometimes the "here" existed only within the scalloped borders of a stamp, as in the work of New Jersey artist Donald Evans. Born in 1945, Evans became fascinated with stamps at an early age. After summers spent building miniature worlds out of sand and cardboard with a friend, he began creating stamps for imaginary lands, complete with census information on the lands' imaginary inhabitants. He would return to this project again in his twenties, eventually designing four thousand stamps from almost one hundred invented lands in a muted watercolor palette of sherbet and sky.

Evans's countries were named after friends' first and last names (Yteke, Adjudani), songs ("My Bonnie" land named for "My Bonnie lies over the ocean"), and abstract concepts, as in the lands of Amis and Amants, which consist of a four-island archipelago based on friendship and love. Each island was named (in French) for a kind of love: Puppy Love, Fair Weather Friend, Hand in Hand, and Lost Love. Other lands were named for food; one example is Mangiare, which has a round-table government and includes Finochiona and Mortadella, two landscapes named for sausages, and the church of St. Haricot Bean. Mangiare contains within its omnivorous borders an autonomous area called "Pasta," divided into twenty-five provinces, "each boasting an example of its namesake noodle on its official coat of arms."[7] Evans wrote of his project, "To my knowledge there are no artists who make stamps in the way I do. But there very well may be. It's like the question of whether we are the only planet in the universe with people on it. I just don't think we are. . . . The stamps are a kind of diary or journal. . . . It's vicarious traveling for me to a made-up world that I like better than the one I'm in. No catastrophes occur. There are no generals or battles or warplanes on my stamps. The countries are innocent, peaceful, composed."[8] The countries are composed as in *tranquil,* and composed as in *created*—in "Pasta," the closest thing to bloodshed would be marinara sauce ladled over the land.

Evans was very invested in his stamps looking "real." He sometimes carved out rubber stamps with an Exacto knife to make it look like the stamps had traveled through various post offices, or he artificially aged them. When he finished a stamp or set of stamps, he "arranged the piece . . . in the plastic pockets of the black stock sheets. . . . He liked them because they were real stamp collectors' sheets and because the black background disguised the typewritten periods he used instead of punched holes to resemble perforations."[9] Thus he made the divide between the real world and his made-up ones all the narrower by putting the imaginary in the wrapper of the real. There's something poignant about the periods standing in for perforation (he meticulously typed "7 1/2 [periods] every two centimeters according to the standard philatelic perforation gauge")—that what should have made it possible for the stamp to be ripped from its sheet and put on a letter was actually the punctuation mark that signals the end of a sentence or thought.[10] The stamps were indeed the end point of Evans's imaginative journeys. They couldn't actually be sent.

Evans moved to Holland in 1972 and, after visiting the town of Stein and drawing some actual views from the town, he created a country of the same name, with Gertrude Stein as its patron saint. He described the land of Stein as a literary dictatorship with 100 percent literacy where the unit of currency was a Gertrude of one hundred cents. One set of stamps used text from Stein's food poems in *Tender Buttons* (imaginary worlds often seem to circle the issue of food like a hungry dinner guest at the buffet table). Another reproduced a section from the poem "A Valentine to Sherwood Anderson" called "Let Us Describe," about an arduous imaginary journey:

Let us describe how they went. It was a very windy night and the road although in excellent condition and extremely well graded has many turnings and although the curves are not sharp the rise is considerable. It was a very windy night and some of the larger vehicles found it more prudent not to venture. In consequence some of those who had planned to go were unable to do so. Many others did go and there was a sacrifice, of what shall we, a sheep, a hen, a cock, a village, a ruin, and all that and then that having been blessed let us bless it.[11]

Unlike the larger vehicles, the stamps could make it on this journey; indeed they carry the text of the journey happily on their little backs. The substitution of text for image on the stamps is an interesting one, implying that the message is so urgent that it has to be placed where it can be read by everyone—on the outside, rather than the inside, of an envelope.

A footnote: Evans suffered from chronic pneumonia and in 1973 doctors discovered that Evans had a third lung. He was advised to have it removed and he channeled his fears about this operation into the creation of Lichaam and Geest (Body and Soul), "twin kingdoms he imagined had once been invaded by ferocious killer whales."[12] He also made the envelope onto which the stamps were affixed into a "disaster cover," or "a piece of mail that has survived a fire, wreck or other calamity and is eventually delivered."[13] It seems extraordinary that someone with so much inspiration (i.e., the dictionary definition: "to infuse some thought or feeling into a person etc. as if by breathing, to animate or actuate") should have had an extra lung. It's as if his two lungs breathed in the air of this world and the third the air of the other, imaginary ones. Four years after the operation, Evans died—presumably of asphyxiation—in a fire in Holland.

Each Rung Has a Rule, or Having Your Head in the Clouds

The first imaginary worlds I visited as a child were in a series of books by Enid Blyton: *The Enchanted Wood, The Magic Faraway Tree,* and *The Folk of the Faraway Tree.* These three stories center on four children who discover a magic tree in an enchanted forest. At the top of the tree, through a ladder in the clouds, different lands come to visit:

> 'Look!' said Jo, in amazement. 'This cloud has a hole in it— and the branches go up—and I believe we're at the very top of the tree! Shall we creep through the cloud-hole and see what land is above?' . . . The branch came to an end and a little ladder ran through the cloud. Up the children went—and before they knew what had happened, there they were out in the sunshine, in a new and very strange land.[14]

Getting to these lands is not an easy matter and looking back on the difficulties the children go through to ascend the tree— inching past Dame Washalot's laundry waterfalls, having to tiptoe past the Angry Pixie's window lest he throw ink on them—they seem to be embodied metaphors for the barriers the world puts in the way of the imagination, and exiting this world. Are you more productive if you do the laundry or if you spend a day with your head in the clouds, allowing imaginary worlds to circle through? To get liftoff, you need to be a little removed from the regular ground, which is perhaps why I liked to read the stories about the Faraway Tree while sitting in the branches of my own sadly earthbound apple tree.

The lands at the top of the tree are structured around one idea, as their names indicate—the land of do as you please, the land of enchantments, the land of treats, the land of dreams, the land of goodies, the land of the topsy turvy, the land of spells, the land of know-alls, the land of tea-parties, the nursery rhyme land, the roundabout land, the land of take-what-you-want, the land of birthdays, and the land of secrets. These lands are extremely rule-bound, offering a manageable amount of mystery. It's possible to extrapolate most of what they contain simply from their names. The land of enchantments even comes with a specific list of rules:

Don't step into a ring drawn on the ground in chalk.

Don't stroke any black cat with green eyes.

Don't be rude to anyone in this land.[15]

Compare this set to the rules of English grammar, your health-care manual, or any of the thousands of unwritten and written rules we live with, and you can see the appeal of inventing a few clear rules within which to live imaginatively. Such utopian worlds have their delights and their limitations. Italo Calvino (whose imaginary worlds we'll look at later) describes them this way: "They come to us as mechanisms that function perfectly in every cogwheel, self-sufficient, self-regulating, and self-reducing."[16]

Imaginary worlds in children's books often strive to create utopias within their rule-bound parameters—they're delicate trees wrapped in burlap sacks and tied with rope so that they'll make it through winter. Creating perfect imaginary worlds—even if they are merely perfect within their own logic—sometimes means only caring about hitting the bull's-eye, whereas the entire dartboard interests me, as does the constellation of pinpoints on the wall around the dartboard made from missing the board entirely.

One-Trick Ponies and Other Self-Important Points

Just one inversion or rule-change can create an entirely alien world. For example, Swiss artist Pippilotti Rist's *Fliegendes Zimmer*, or *Flying Room*, in which a chair, a table, and a little oriental rug float upside down, close to the ceiling, implies a weakening of gravity and an inverted world. We can extrapolate from this glimpse to scenes of cars driving along the undersides of clouds. Similarly, in eighteenth-century writer Nicolas de la Bretonne's "Megapatagonia," an imaginary locale that is geographically exactly opposite France, "the inhabitants speak an inversion of French—for instance, 'Good day' is '*Nob ruoj*.' They wear shoes on their heads and hats on their feet."[17] Russell Edson, in his poem "Antimatter," creates a world in which every rule is inverted:

> On the other side of the mirror there's an inverse world, where the insane go sane; where bones climb out of the earth and recede to the first slime of love.
> And in the evening the sun is just rising.

Lovers cry because they are a day younger, and soon childhood robs them of their pleasure.

In such a world there is much sadness which, of course, is
joy.[18]

In *Haroun and the Sea of Stories*, Salman Rushdie invents
and organizes a city based on one thing—sadness—which seeps
into every last nook: "There was once, in the country of Alifbay,
a sad city, the saddest of cities, a city so ruinously sad that it had
forgotten its name. It stood by a mournful sea full of glumfish,
which were so miserable to eat that they made people belch with
melancholy even though the skies were blue. In the north of the
sad city stood mighty factories in which (so I'm told) sadness
was actually manufactured, packaged and sent all over the world,
which never seemed to get enough of it."[19] Thus the city's sadness permeates the people's mood, their diet, even what they ex-
port. Perhaps it is worth noting that the one family that doesn't
suffer from the general gloom is the family with a storyteller as
its patriarch—someone who endlessly invents worlds.

The reduction used in the creation of imaginary worlds
sometimes takes the form of literally decreased dimensionality.
Edwin A. Abbott's *Flatland: A Romance of Many Dimensions*,
published in 1884, explores the notion of a one-, two-, three-,
and four-dimensional world. At one point (pun intended) the
narrator, Mr. A. Square who lives in 2-D, visits Pointland and
gets to have an overarching perspective over a world that is less
complex than his. Pointland consists of one charmingly self-
absorbed point who cannot conceive of a world outside himself
and talks to himself all day in the following manner: "It fills all

Space . . . and what It fills, It is. What It thinks, that It utters; and what It utters, that It hears; and It itself is Thinker, Utterer, Hearer, Thought, Word, Audition; it is the One, and yet the All in All. Ah, the happiness, ah, the happiness of Being!"[20]

In Italo Calvino's story "All at One Point," we see a world that is first cousin to the point in Pointland—not that he would ever know it. Calvino's point world exists at "the moment when all of the universe's matter was concentrated in a single point, before it began to expand in space."[21] He constructs a tale about neighbors who live on top of each other, literally. This makes for some strange bedfellows: when the much-desired Mrs. Ph(i)Nko has sex with her male friend, for instance, she is actually having sex with everyone in the land. The situation is comic, but there's a bitter biscuit beneath the pink icing: in Calvino's preworld world all our prejudices and divisions preexist. For example, despite the fact that there is no possible cleaning to be done—"inside one point not even a grain of dust can enter"—there is a cleaning woman representing the working class.[22] Then there is the Z-zu family, who most in the land treat as lowly immigrants despite the fact that "neither before nor after existed, nor any place to immigrate from."[23] By condensing the world Calvino lassos all its faults into one tiny corral where they're very easy to see trotting around self-importantly.

Climbing Up the Dimensional Ladder, or 2-D Glasses and One-Liners

A. Square's native abode, Flatland, adds a dimension to the story and more cultural complexity to boot. Flatland is an extremely rule- and ruler-bound world where "the greatest length or breadth of a full-grown inhabitant of Flatland may be estimated at about eleven of your inches."[24] The inhabitants are different shapes according to their social status. Women—lowest on the social ladder—are straight lines, and resemble a rung. Male servants and soldiers are isosceles triangles, the male middle class are equilateral triangles, and professional men and gentlemen like A. Square are squares or pentagons. Finally, the nobility range from hexagons to polygons, and the priests have so many sides that they approach—but never reach—the perfection of the circle.

The rules are as follows: "It is a Law of Nature with us that a male child shall have one more side than his father, so that each generation shall rise (as a rule) one step in the scale of development and nobility. Thus the son of a Square is a Pentagon; the son of a Pentagon, a Hexagon; and so on."[25] Thus upward mobility is built into the system and the addition of a new male to the family line is translated into the addition of a line to the child's shape. A. Square goes on to note that this rule only applies to the middle class and above. An isosceles father will therefore almost always have an isosceles child, though in rare cases isosceles parents will produce an equilateral child—thus incorporating the smallest smidgen of the possibility of upward mobility for the working classes. The government has rules to govern even this situation—that infant is examined and if confirmed as being "Regular," he is "immediately taken from his proud yet sorrowing parents and adopted by some childless Equilateral" and never allowed to see his parents again.[26]

The inhabitants of Flatland also have an elaborate system of determining class and gender of the person they are speaking to via voice recognition and "feeling" each other, an extremely rule-bound operation in which one person "feels" and infers one of the angles of another person. Because women are only lines, they disappear if you are right in front or right behind them and could accidentally pierce a male subject—so "no female is suffered to stand in any public place without swaying her back from right to left."[27] An extremely dignified solution . . .

With his 2-D tongue firmly in his 2-D cheek, A. Square is clearly commenting on issues of class and gender in his native England. As dimensions increase, so do the social structures. Pointland is purely solipsistic; Lineland (distinct from Flatland in that everything in the world is along one line) satirizes a narrow viewpoint or one-track mind, and Flatland gives us the blueprints (complete with dimensions) for the inequalities of the real world. When A. Square is taken to the world of 3-D (which he calls "Space World"), he gets an even clearer view of his governmentally determined and prescribed hexagonal house, his hexagonal sons in their rooms, the isosceles shapes of the pages, the scullion, the footman, and the butler, and the insignificant line segments that are his wife and daughter.

Anne or (A.) Carson seems to be writing, if not living, along a similar line to A. Square. In the introduction to her series of thirty-six poems, "The Life of Towns," she writes:

> I am a scholar of towns, let God commend that. To explain what I do is simple enough. A scholar is someone who takes a position. From which position, certain lines become visible. You will at first think I am painting the lines myself; it's not so. I merely know where to stand to see the lines that are there.

And the mysterious thing, it is a very mysterious thing, is how these lines do paint themselves. Before there were any edges or angles or virtue—who was there to ask the questions? Well, let's not get carried away with exegesis. A scholar is someone who knows how to limit himself to the matter at hand. Matter which has painted itself within lines constitutes a town.[28]

The towns that Carson describes are practically one-liners, with the title as the setup, and the poem as the punch line. Like A. Square, she seems to see the towns she writes about from above—the city limits are made visible in the titles. Perhaps she is also pointing to the limits of scholarship.

In "September Town," Carson addresses the danger of 2-Deifying in a 3-D world:

One fear is that.
The sound of cicadas.
Out in the blackness zone is going to crush my head.
Flat as a piece of paper some night then.
I'll be expected.
To go ahead with normal tasks.
Mending the screen.
Door hiding my.
Brother from the police.[29]

The town is walled off by date: with an entrance gate at the first of September and no exit gate for the thirtieth, this town is permanently in the year's ninth month, a time of transition. The poem consists of one elaborate fear—that the sound of the cicadas will flatten the speaker's head, a physical manifestation of insanity. This fits well in terms of dimensionality—the speaker is scared to lose all depth and then, despite her condition, still be expected to do the things she considers "normal" (i.e., repairing a screen door and screening her brother from the police). Mending the screen door seems the more possible task with a 2-D head, but "hiding my. / Brother from the police" would seem to require more cunning. If her head is flattened, is her world flattened also? You can only hide things in a 3-D world. As in Flatland, a cupboard wouldn't hide anyone if the police were in 3-D—the brother would be right there in the floor plan. The town is flat on the page in its textual incarnation, so we see him sitting there on the last line. There's no point in trying to hide him from us or the police.

Stylistically, all of Carson's town poems use the device of breaking up sentences by putting a period at the end of each line regardless of syntax. In this poem, the punctuation forces the lines to stand alone in 2-D, before they accrue a third dimension by continuing on down the page. The periods create a door that screens the line from what follows it, but one that syntax pushes open.

"Memory Town" presents the reverse situation—the speaker is painting a picture (primarily a 2-D pursuit) when a third dimension seems to open up:

In each one of you I paint.
I find.
A buried site of radioactive material.
You think 8 miles down is enough?
15 miles?
140 miles?[30]

Here the surface of the 2-D canvas develops a depth, a 3-D portal, like the ship portrait at the beginning of C. S. Lewis's *The Voyage of the Dawn Treader*. In this third book in the Narnia series Edmund, Lucy, and Eustace are looking at a painting when suddenly they find themselves swimming inside the once-painted sea next to the ship. Suddenly reality can be found inside the frame.[31] In "Memory Town," again dimensionality creates conflict. The radioactive material is miles underground but still affects the surface visible to the painter of these memory towns. The three insistent questions point to a desire to make the radioactive memories disappear completely, yet the distance needed to sever the town itself from its memories seems increasingly unattainable. Perhaps Memory Town is a ghost town, steeped in the past.

Visible Sources, or Dissection, Gestation, and the Aerial View

Further down the road of Calvino's career, one finds his book *Invisible Cities*, which consists of lyrical travel reports delivered by Marco Polo to the emperor Kublai Khan. Marco Polo describes these cities as a foreigner might—trying to find the rules of each place around which the cities cohere in a way that will make the city most visible to Kublai Khan and the reader. The book is highly structured—the fifty-five cities are divided into nine sections, and each city is identified not by its name but by one of eleven appellations: "cities and memory," "cities and desire," "cities and signs," "thin cities," "trading cities," "cities and eyes," "cities and names," "cities and the dead," "cities and the sky," "continuous cities," and "hidden cities," with five cities in each category.

The city of Baucis, built on stilts so tall that the city is up beyond the cloud layer, seems to speak to the reasons for creating imaginary worlds. Calvino writes of the city's separation from terra firma: "There are three hypotheses about the inhabitants of Baucis: that they hate the earth; that they respect it so much they avoid all contact; that they love it as it was before they existed and with spyglasses and telescopes aimed downward they never tire of examining it, leaf by leaf, stone by stone, ant by ant, contemplating with fascination their own absence."[32] The near-invisible stilts are a wonderful metaphor for how our invented worlds never let us fully leave the world we live in. As Frederico García Lorca put it, "the imagination is limited by reality: one cannot imagine what does not exist. It needs objects, landscapes, planets, and it requires the purest sort of logic to relate those things to one another. One cannot leap into the abyss or do away with terms of reality. Imagination has horizons, it wants to delineate and make concrete all that lies within its reach. . . . The imagination hovers over reason the way fragrance hovers over a flower, without detaching itself from the petals, wafted on the breeze but tied, always, to the ineffable center of its origin."[33]

Calvino's city of Armilla is a dissected world that "has nothing that makes it seem a city, except the water pipes that rise vertically where the houses should be and spread out horizontally where the floors should be: a forest of pipes that end in taps, showers, spouts, overflows."[34] Armilla is reminiscent of artist Nina Katchadourian's dissected road and subway maps, which she cuts out of preexisting maps and turns into delicate spiderwebs—pieces that reveal the different systems and structures within each city, the dendrites of electricity that spark under- and aboveground, the circulatory system of subway tunnels and bus routes with all the meat and madness of the roads and buildings and life stripped away. In her piece *Austria*, which is only 5 x 7 inches, Katchadourian has shaped the network of highways into the shape of a heart, referencing both Austria's role as the "heart of Europe" and the way her pieces evoke the human circulatory system.[35]

When Calvino strips away everything except for the water pipes, lifting them out of a preexisting world like a spiderweb carefully removed from a tree, he allows for a new minimal but magical city to emerge—one that doesn't have the multiplicity and complexity of a real city. This magic in turn seems to conjure up Armilla's otherworldly inhabitants, the nymphs and naiads—who can be seen "luxuriating in the bathtubs or arching their backs under the showers suspended in the void" as if they themselves sprang from those shower nozzles, those gleaming faucets.[36]

Another city, "Olinda," proceeds on a model of infinite growth and reproduction. In Olinda, a miniature city is always found gestating within the "mother" city, like the micronations that are found embedded within an existing country. Australia is currently home to a number of such micronations—The Hutt River Principality, the Province of Bumbunga, the Independent State of Rainbow Creek, Atlantium, the Principality of Marlborough, and the Principality of United Oceania—little joeys in the pouch of the mother kangaroo. Some take the form of a farm or a group of farms; others exist within the walls of an apartment. But Olinda's micronations endlessly and alarmingly proliferate and expand. In describing these tiny worlds within worlds pushing the older versions farther and farther from the center, Calvino compares the process to known natural imagery such as the concentric rings seen in tree trunks, and these references provide us with stilts strong enough that we could slide down them and land in our world of trees and flowers and bodies. Indeed, every imaginary world bears the faint watermark of planet earth if you hold the map up to the light of examination.

Organ Music, or Whereupon the Trail Leads into the Entrails

As children, the world expands concentrically. There's the discovery of me, then the house, the trees outside it, countries, continents, planets. It follows then that in inventing new worlds we often turn to our original material, our first abode, the body. In Peter Blegvad's comic *The Book of Leviathan*, we see the baby protagonist's anthropomorphic map in which his parents are continent-sized and cookies and xylophones constitute countries. Leviathan's version of the world has only a slightly greater circumference than that of Abbot's Pointland. Joost de Momper, a Flemish artist whose life bridged the sixteenth and seventeenth centuries, painted *Spring* and *Summer*, landscapes in which rock formations form two craggy busts. Each has a different treeline hairstyle, one has a castle nose. Momper uses the body as his building material, creating two father, instead of mother, earths.

Terrance Hayes's charming love poem "Preface" (cleverly punning on the notion of the brain being behind and therefore pre-face) swoops inside his lover's head and finds a world there:

Well, ain't your mouth a pretty little pace-
maker. And *mmmm* that tongue is a carp
I'd sure like to harpoon! We could eat crêpe-
suzettes in the dim café
below your hypothalamus. I'd pull the last pear
from the pear tree. We could peer
over the ridge of your throat or creep
down the ladder until we reached the reef.
But before setting forth, you should accept whatever's free
because, Baby, I've got at least one acre
of desires you can reap.[37]

Here we witness the jump into otherworldliness via metaphor. The mouth is called a "pace-maker," the tongue "a carp,"
and then, at this point, the speaker takes the full plunge and
lands in the "dim café" below the hypothalamus. By the end of
the poem, the speaker's body has become a landscape also, re-
plete with "one acre / of desires." This poem adopts the inverse
of Momper's paintings as strategy—Momper makes the outside
world reflect the human form; Hayes makes the interior of the
body reflect the outside world.

Moving farther down the body, we land in one of Henri Michaux's imaginary human landscapes (access to which was often
provided by a mescaline visa). In the Land of Magic is an area
where the stomach is extruded onto the landscape:

"The Stomach (the stomach-province) was used against en-
emies from the West. . . . When they came down into the plain,
these mountain people had to cross a river. Their feet were

digested. . . . The whole region before them had been trans-formed into a stomach: that is the truth of the matter. . . . Eaten up, not by leprosy, but by the awful juices of the Stomach, nearly all of them perished.[38]

Like Rushdie's sad city, every element of this landscape—the ground, the weather, the very atmosphere—is infused with stomach-ness. This is a land with one aim and one aim only: digestion of whoever dares to enter it. Which is not exactly what Calvino was talking about when he described utopia "not as a city that can be founded by us but that can found itself in us, build itself brick by brick in our ability to imagine it, to think it out to the ultimate degree; a city that claims to inhabit us, not to be inhabited"—but then, would he really police the barrier between the literal and the figurative?[39] I think he might well allow it to be permeable like the intestinal wall, allowing food molecules to pass through it and enter the bloodstream.

Surrealism as Escape Vehicle, or Island Hors d'Oeuvres

So that we may pass through the perilous stomach-province without being digested ourselves, permit me to offer up to it Pastemolle, "a small perfectly round island in the undefined region of the Fortunate Islands" invented by an anonymous French author in 1538.[40] The only means of access is through a gateway of melted cheese, dried in the sun until it has become harder than steel. Pastemolle is surrounded by ovens, with their backs to the sea, constantly full of various types of pies. For the convenience of visitors, notices above the ovens specify which type of pie is produced by which oven. The island is the home of a colony of extremely devout marmots, burrowing rodents of the genus *Arctomys*, who live in a convent."[41]

The marmots in the convent aren't interested in commenting on this world—they're busy burrowing into the one they live in. Pastemolle belongs to a class of imaginary worlds that is more about fancy and escapism, about trying to sever the sense-making ties between real and imaginary worlds. However, just as our heads are attached to our bodies, even the most surreal of worlds have worldly elements to them—pies, marmots, convents. Surrealist Tristan Tzara invented Fluorescente, "a city where, according to the local historian, 'a street-singer puts darkness to a test of silence spread like a pool of red wine,'—a phrase that has a profound meaning in its original language, Dada. The most striking feature is the fruit placed in piles at crossroads throughout the city, some of the piles reaching the height of three-storey buildings. . . . Sounds are muted by spreading a thin layer of rubber over everything that might make a sharp noise. "[42] In Tzara's world the meaning of language changes, but there is still a language. The muting of sound is done in an unusual way, but one that might well work. And the fruit piles, though inexplicable, are plucked from the same trees we find in earth's orchards.

Anne Carson's "One-Man Town" moves away from the real in its nod to the Surrealist movement: "It's Magritte weather today said Max. / Ernst knocking his head on a boulder."[43] The boulder Ernst knocks his head against is found in numerous paintings by Magritte, thereby combining the contradictory one-liner couplet poem with the master of the double-take. But

Carson makes "One-Man Town" even more contradictory. The town supposedly has a sole inhabitant but two men are referred to. As in all the town poems, the lines end with periods—so the name and surname "Max Ernst" also registers as two male first names, adding a potential third. The period, combined with the line break, also enacts the injury—the boulder hits both poem and person in the head.

Magritte's floating-boulder paintings investigate a number of possible hierarchies involving the boulder and the landscape. *Les Idées claires* or *Clear Ideas* (1958) shows a sea with a boulder floating above it and a cloud floating directly above the boulder. In *La Bataille de l'Argonne* or *The Battle of the Argonne* (1959), the cloud and boulder are floating side by side over a stripe of landscape and above them both is a sliver of moon, a much larger chunk of rock. In *Le Château des Pyrénnées* or *The Castle in the Pyrenees* (1959), the boulder takes center stage, dominating the picture plane a few inches above another stripe of sea, this time with a stone castle rising from its top. Carson also inserts a person into the hitherto unpopulated hierarchy, a person who in "knocking his head on a boulder" seems on the same level as the boulder, equivalent like the cloud.

It's like gravity: we can only jump so high before we fall back to earth. Part of me finds this disappointing—I'd like to believe that the imagination could invent something wholly other. Still, there are encouragingly strange developments in the real world. For example, string theory now posits that there are ten or eleven dimensions, not three, so we are far, far beyond Abbott's smug little point. The planet Mercury was considered the smallest planet in our solar system until the 1930 discovery of

Pluto. On November 14, 2003, three scientists discovered another planet candidate named Sedna that is smaller than Pluto and farther from the sun. It is currently ninety-three million miles away and has a diameter of approximately one thousand miles and, very possibly, its own moon. Dr. Chad Trujillo of the Gemini Observatory in Hawaii was quoted as saying, "We still don't understand what is on the surface of this body. It is nothing like what we would have predicted or what we can currently explain."[44]

Time Travel and Globe Heads

If we travel along the dimension of time back to 1749, the balls of mercury that spilled at the start of this essay re-form their silver stream and slip back into their reconstituted glass thermometer casing, float from the floor back into the hand and can be used in Denis Diderot's "Thermometer Island," located "somewhere in the Atlantic Ocean, so-called because the laws of the country allow couples to sleep with each other only if the sexes of both husband and wife, measured with special thermometers, have reached the same temperatures."[45] Another, slightly less intrusive feature of the island is that "the islanders are born with the visible signs of their vocation: in this way each one is what he should be. Those destined to the science of geometry are born with fingers in the form of a compass; someone who is to be an astronomer is born with eyes in the form of telescopes; geographers are born with heads like terrestrial globes. "[46] In my view, all of us have globes perched on our neat little neck-stands and

equatorial grins above our chins, which means we're all potential inventor-geographers, particularly writers. Every time we
put pen to paper we're inventing a world—one whose rules get
made up as we go along. Poems and stories inhabit that unstable
place of creation—you, the writer, are ostensibly in charge but
then a character you've created tosses the narrative frisbee into a
nearby field, an image sidles up to a lyric stream, impatient to be
transformed into a fish, a bit of dialogue begs for a dance partner
to rhyme with. And as we write, a world appears, coheres, takes
on colors and questions, cities and certainties.

NOTES

1. A marvelous collection of these worlds can be found in *The Dictionary
of Imaginary Places* compiled by Alberto Manguel and Gianni Guadalupi.
It is a book that by all rights should refuse its mundane seat assignment
next to the thesaurus on the bookcase and instead float up to the ceiling for
a tête-à-tête with an imaginary chandelier. Perhaps the book is as heavy as
it is to prevent such problems for the reader. After reading it I sometimes
found it a bit difficult to come back to planet earth and, when I did, I was
prone to seeing suns in lightbulbs, ravioli as islands floating in a sage-butter
ocean, and solar systems circling my wrist in the form of a bracelet.

2. *Paper Bodies: A Margaret Cavendish Reader*, edited by Sylvia
Bowerbank and Sara Mendelson (Toronto: Broadview Literary Texts,
2000), 212–13.

3. http://micronations.wikia.com/wiki/Micronation

4. Perhaps it stands to reason that amoebas, some of that sludge's first
citizens, were amorphous and flexible about their own boundaries. The
first borders often followed divisions that existed in the land—rivers and
mountains created natural boundaries and lent legitimacy and inevitability
to the project of dividing up the land.

5. *The Best of the Prose Poem: An International Journal*, edited by Peter Johnson (Buffalo: White Pine Press, 2000), 29.

6. Only two of her poems have been translated into English, and both by Gary Sea, spelled S-E-A. So the message of this poem actually went via the sea to get to me.

7. Eisenhart, Willy, *The World of Donald Evans* (New York: Abbeville Press, 1994), 126.

8. Donald Evans, interview in *The Paris Review*, Summer 1975.

9. Eisenhart, *The World of Donald Evans*, 17.

10. Ibid., 19.

11. Ibid., 137.

12. Ibid., 16.

13. Ibid., 90.

14. Blyton, Enid, *The Enchanted Wood* (London: Purnell and Sons, 1939), 30–31.

15. Ibid., 125.

16. Calvino, Italo, *The Uses of Literature* (New York: Harcourt Brace Company, 1982), 245–46.

17. De la Bretonne, Nicolas-Edme Restif, La Découverte australe Par un Homme-volant, ou Le Dédale français; Nouvelle très-philosophique: Suivie de la Lettre d un Singe, &ca, Leipzig, 1781, from *The Dictionary of Imginary Places*, edited by Alberto Manguel and Gianni Guadallupi (New York: Harcourt, 2000), 226.

18. Edson, Russel, *The Tunnel: Selected Poems* (Oberlin: Oberlin College Press, 1944), 125.

19. Rushdie, Salman, *Haroun and the Sea of Stories* (London: Granta Books, 1990), 15.

20. Abbott, Edwin A., *Flatland: A Romance of Many Dimensions* (New York: Dover Publications, 1992), 76.

21. Calvino, Italo, "All at One Point," in *Fantastic Worlds, Myths, Tales, and Stories*, edited by Eric S. Rabkin (Oxford: Oxford University Press, 1979), 438.

22. Ibid., 439.

23. Ibid.

24. Abbott, *Flatland*, 7.

25. Ibid., 7.

26. Ibid., 8.

27. Ibid., 12.

28. Carson, Anne, *Plainwater* (New York: Alfred A. Knopf, 1995), 93.

29. Ibid., 100.

30. Ibid., 101.

31. The inverse of this scenario can be found in the 2003 animated feature film *The Triplets of Belleville*, written and directed by Sylvain Chomet. Three bicyclists have been kidnapped from an equivalent of the Tour de France by the French mafia and are forced to race each other on stationary bicycles in front of a flickering film of a landscape. When the hero's grandmother finds him and the one other surviving bicyclist and unscrews the platform on which they are racing from the floor, we get a wonderful scene of the entire contraption racing through the streets. The cyclists are now cycling through a real landscape but are still only looking at the filmed one in front of them, an interesting interpretation of the old adage about "taking art to the streets."

32. Calvino, Italo, *Invisible Cities* (New York: Harcourt, 1972), 77.

33. García Lorca, Frederico, "Imagination, Inspiration and Evasion," *jubilat* 7: 2004, 48.

34. Calvino, *Invisible Cities*, 49.

35. Harmon, Katherine, *You Are Here: Personal Geographies and Other Maps of the Imagination* (New York: Princeton Architectural Press, 2004), 77.

36. Calvino, *Invisible Cities*, 49.

37. Hayes, Terrance, *Hip Logic* (New York: Penguin, 2002), 66.

38. *Darkness Moves: An Henri Michaux Anthology: 1927–1984*, selected and translated by David Ball (Berkeley: University of California Press, 1994), 125–26.

39. Calvino, *The Uses of Literarture*, 252.

40. Anonymous, Le Voyage de navigation que fist Panurge, disciple de Pantagruel, aux isles incongnues et èstranges de plusiers choses merveilleuses et difficiles à croire, qu il dict avoir veues, dont il fait narration en ce présent volume, et plusiers aultres joyeusetez pour inciter les lecteurs et audieteurs à rire, Paris, 1538, from *The Dictionary of Imaginary Places*, 511.

41. Ibid.

42. Tzara, Tristan, *Grains et Issues,* Paris, 1935, from *The Dictionary of Imaginary Places,* 226.

43. Carson, *Plainwater,* 105.

44. www.nasa.gov/vision/universe/solarsystem/planet_like_body.html

45. Diderot, Denis, *Les Bijoux indiscrets,* from *The Dictionary of Imaginary Places,* 647.

46. Ibid.

MAKING A SCENE
Fiction's Fundamental Unit

ANNA KEESEY

WHAT IS A SCENE? On a particular hypothetical occasion, in a particular hypothetical place, we see enacted in front of us events and behaviors. These flow continuously until there is a break in time or a shift of place. This is the conventional definition. But what's the context? If this is a scene, what do you call all that stuff on the page that's not scene? And what are the variations within scenes? How can they be constructed?

Usually, when we talk about fiction, we come at it from sexier standpoints. We talk about how significant detail creates character, how character creates conflict, how conflict manifests action, and how all commingle to produce an expression of theme. To look solely at the forms, or subforms, really, of fiction—the Legos that snap together—can seem geeky, unappreciative of the dynamism and flow and systemic beauty of good storytelling. But it seems to me useful for beginning writers to think about these Legos prior to those intense working moments when they are trying both to imagine a world *and* to render it.

Part of what makes writing fiction so difficult is that the writer must decide what's going to happen, to whom, and why, but is simultaneously loaded up with another set of decisions: who'll be telling the story, in what order, with what level of detail and at what speed of revelation. The narrative theorists who mull and write on these issues, and to whom I am indebted for these ideas, people like Seymour Chatman and Mieke Bal and H. Porter Abbot, call these two worlds of choices *story* and *discourse*: *story* is what happens to your unfortunate characters; *discourse* is the way you, the writer, present it to your reader. What happens and how it's rendered; the what of it and the way of it. So when you're sitting there at your computer weeping, trying to figure something out, shore yourself up with the knowledge that what you're trying to figure out could belong to the world of story or to the world of discourse or to some nexus of the two, and it's just not easy to do.

So let's break it down. For now we'll leave *story* up to you —that's for you to determine in the shower or while drunk—but let's consider the most important *discourse* decision you have to make. This concerns what to *show* and what to *tell about*—and will lead you to an understanding of scene.

Let's examine a familiar narrative in terms of the discourse decisions made by the storyteller. This is the King James Bible, book of Genesis, chapter three, verses one through eight:

> Now the serpent was more subtil than any beast of the field which the LORD God had made. And he said unto the woman, Yea, hath God said, Ye shall not eat of every tree of the garden? And the woman said unto the serpent, We may eat of the fruit

of the trees of the garden: But of the fruit of the tree which is in the midst of the garden, God hath said, Ye shall not eat of it, neither shall ye touch it, lest ye die. And the serpent said unto the woman, Ye shall not surely die: For God doth know that in the day ye eat thereof, then your eyes shall be opened, and ye shall be as gods, knowing good and evil.

And when the woman saw that the tree was good for food, and that it was pleasant to the eyes, and a tree to be desired to make one wise, she took of the fruit thereof, and did eat, and gave also unto her husband with her; and he did eat. And the eyes of them both were opened, and they knew that they were naked; and they sewed fig leaves together, and made themselves aprons. And they heard the voice of the LORD God walking in the garden in the cool of the day: and Adam and his wife hid themselves from the presence of the LORD God amongst the trees of the garden.

When we recover from yet another encounter with our inheritance of sin and our natural curiosity about what the aprons looked like and whether they in fact tied at the small of the back, we notice something peculiar. Here we are in the ur-moment in the ur-text of Western civilization. We expect a unified narrative, a pure narrative, an unbroken utterance of equally weighted events. But what do we notice? Discourse decisions! The shown and the told! Scene and summary!

Let me explain. We hear Eve's conversation with the serpent in real time—he speaks, she speaks, he speaks, and so on, and what's rendered there on the page takes essentially the same amount of time to transpire as it would in life. But the rest of the actions—Eve eating and tempting Adam, Adam eating, eyes opened, nakedness, shame, figs, aprons, God, the miscreants secreting themselves in the arborvitae hedge—which would consume a much greater amount of time than the initial conversation, take up about the same amount of space on the page. What's the difference here? Eve's interview with the serpent would take a certain amount of time to transpire in the physical world, and that amount of hypothetical time is here devoted to the rendering of it; that is to say, story time is equal to discourse time (st = dt). This is *scene*. In the rest of the passage, however, story time is greater than discourse time—it would take *longer* to transpire in life than the time devoted to its rendering—and we call that *summary* (st > dt). Now, the summary mode can be very involving in its own way, particularly because of the breathtaking speed with which fictional events can unfold, so I'm not weighting scene over summary in terms of absolute value to the writer or reader. But unlike scene, summary places an extra layer of distance between the reader and the action. The reader doesn't observe the events happening. Somebody else observed all that business in the garden that afternoon and compressed time in the recounting of it; the action is filtered and reduced.

You'll note that these distinctions roughly correspond to the fiction writer's maxim "Show, don't tell." *Scene* shows; *summary* tells. You may be thinking, "Sweet. When I get to the big workshop in the sky, I'll be able to say to God, 'Maybe it's just me, but Genesis 3:6–8? Show, don't tell, dawg.'" This of course might be a bit rash, because Dawg will surely remind you that there are plenty of examples of scene that slip by almost as quickly as summary, and plenty of summary as bejeweled with detail as a patient scene. But the basic point is valid: Eve and the serpent get more airtime. We watch them more closely. Their conversation unfolds beat by real-time beat. So the discourse choices the writer has made—what to render in scene and what in summary—have the effect of, at the very least, shining a brighter light on the disgrace of Eve than that of Adam.

In his classic text *The Art of Fiction,* John Gardner talks about the fictional dream, which is a kind of trance—I consider it a sacred one—in which people read and they forget they're reading and they see the thing in front of them as though it's actually happening. They drop through the letters on the page into the imagined worlds and they respond to that world emotionally as if its events are actually happening. This is mystical, this is amazing, isn't it? We can read letters—hieroglyphics—that form words on the page, and the words refer symbolically to invented people and invented action, and yet we weep as if these people were real, and our loved ones.

And the scene, the action played out in front of us, gives us that feeling and puts us in that trance more than any other mode of fiction. We see the action occur; we feel the time pass. Like the scene on the dramatic stage and in cinema, the written scene carries the feeling of immediacy. Im-mediate: *not mediated by another.* To speak technically, a fictional scene is *not* unmediated because there always exists a narrative presence that is choosing the details, but the scene at least engenders the *illusion* of immediacy—the illusion that nobody else is summarizing the action for you and attaching significance to it; we get to see it happen and interpret it ourselves. All other qualities of the fiction being equal, the scene is most trance-inducing, the most transporting and hypnotic.

Having understood that idea, though, let's look at some variations on the scene that are available to you when you're laying it down, when you're discoursing your story. Let's look at Virginia Woolf, one of those writers who push the scene, who stretch it and elongate it such that it becomes something else.

Those who have read Woolf's *To the Lighthouse* will recognize these characters and this dialogue. But I've adapted the original by compiling everything that constitutes an event, everything that progresses time in the narrative, and I've *omitted* everything that does *not* advance story time.

"Yes, of course, if it's fine tomorrow," said Mrs. Ramsay. "But you'll have to be up with the lark," she added. To her son these words conveyed an extraordinary joy.

"But," said his father, stopping in front of the drawing room window, "it won't be fine."

"It may be fine. I expect it will be fine," said Mrs. Ramsay.

"It's due west," said the atheist Tansley, holding his bony fingers spread so that the wind blew through them.

"Nonsense," said Mrs. Ramsay.

"There'll be no landing at the lighthouse, tomorrow," said Tansley.

Three people speak and make gestures. In this adaptation, fewer than one hundred words are used to represent events that might require a minute of real time. But if you know the original, you know that this conversation takes place over twelve closely spaced pages of text. In the original, each of these lines of dialogue is an occasion for the Woolfiness of Woolf, that tremendous deepening and reflection and rhetorical flight in which she is characterizing the people, recalling their pasts, capturing their fleeting physical experiences, illuminating their mental processes and emotions, following the glittering floss of consciousness as it weaves throughout the action.

The acts of speech and gesture and event above, such as Tansley spreading his bony fingers, and Mrs. Ramsay asserting "Nonsense," are nodes of advancement of the story time, the *unfolding* of the story. Yet, in between and simultaneous with any of these moments of the story time passing, there is a tremendous amount of fictional enriching and deepening. I call this "infolding." The scene is "infolded" elaborately, but the story time that elapses is the same as it is in the sparse adaptation. After twelve pages, we arrive at the same moment in time—Tansley's dismissal of the lighthouse plan.

Some writers, like Woolf or Proust, emphasize *infolding* almost to the exclusion of unfolding. Very few events that we consider of present significance occur—discourse time is greater than story time: st < dt. We might call this a stretched scene, an infolded scene, or a slo-mo scene.

Consider yourself, as a writer. When you put your story up for discussion in workshop, people may say, "Wow, it's great. There's so much going on. It's exciting, it's fast. But I just don't really feel like I understand the characters' motivations, and I can't picture the setting." If so, you're probably natively an *unfolder*. Or do people say, "Your language is fabulous and your perceptions are terrific, but, you know, nothing ever happens." You're probably an *infolder*. If it's boom, boom, boom and buildings are blowing up and she bursts in and says, "I'm pregnant," you're an unfolder.

If you have a character who sees a girl on a bus, and she reminds him of another girl he once knew who collected beetles and mounted them on cards, and one of them had an opalescent shell of unearthly blue . . . you're an infolder.

I think that whether you are an unfolder or an infolder has a lot to do with your disposition as a person and as a thinker. Some people are interested in events, in social relationships, in forces and movements exterior to the cranium; for others, consciousness itself is the only real subject matter. Fifty years from now, we'll probably be able to say our infolding Virginia had one type of brain chemistry and Ernest Hemingway, who unfolds like crazy, had another. But the *why* really doesn't signify, because you can be a fabulous writer as an extreme unfolder or as an extreme infolder, and as everything in between. I don't offer this distinction to you as advice as how to *correct* your tendencies—only in order that you can identify and use the skills you have and are developing. In fact, most writers have some kind of combination of these predispositions, these tools, and use them according to the fictional task facing them. Most of us are just groping toward something that feels right and doesn't feel wrong.

We've talked about what fiction looks like when story time is equal to discourse time (scene), greater than discourse time (summary), and less than discourse time (stretch). Here's another equation: frequently, in fiction, discourse time equals zero.

For example, let's look at two micro scenes from the classic Denis Johnson story "Emergency":

> I was hanging out in the E.R. with fat, quivering Nurse. One
> of the Family Service doctors that nobody liked came in looking

for Georgie to wipe up after him. "Where's Georgie?" this guy
asked.

"Georgie's in the O.R.," Nurse said.

"Again?"

"No," Nurse said. "Still."

"Still? Doing What??"

"Cleaning the floor."

"Again?"

"No," Nurse said again. "Still."

Back in O.R., Georgie dropped his mop and bent over in the
posture of a child soiling its diapers. He stared down with his
mouth open in terror.

He said, "What am I going to do about these fucking *shoes*,
man."

Look at that little space between Nurse saying "Still" and
the next paragraph beginning "Back in O.R." The point-of-view
character has had to take his sorry self over to the O.R., yet that
journey is not related. Story time has progressed, but no discourse is devoted to it. So what does discourse time equal? Zero.
Story time is progressing, but there is no discourse beyond a
carriage return and an indention. When story is not rendered
but is only implied, when events are elided, when dt = 0, we call
it *ellipsis*.

Now I want to return to the scene and look at variations
within that mode. Let's look at three, just to see what it is that
they do so variously and beautifully and to help you expand
your repertoire of strategies for moving through them.

Consider "Hills Like White Elephants," probably Hemingway's most well-known short story, which consists essentially of one long scene. A couple sits together in a train station café in Spain, on a hot day in the 1920s. He wants her to do something, and, given her sarcasm and evasions, she doesn't seem to want to do it. We ultimately deduce that she is pregnant and he'd like her to end the pregnancy. Here's a passage:

"Yes," said the girl. "Everything tastes of licorice. Especially all the things you've waited so long for, like absinthe."

"Oh, cut it out."

"You started it," the girl said. "I was being amused. I was having a fine time."

"Well, let's try and have a fine time."

"All right. I was trying. I said the mountains looked like white elephants. Wasn't that bright?"

"That was bright."

"I wanted to try this new drink: That's all we do, isn't it—look at things and try new drinks?"

"I guess so."

The girl looked across at the hills.

"They're lovely hills," she said. "They don't really look like white elephants. I just meant the coloring of their skin through the trees."

"Should we have another drink?"

"All right."

The warm wind blew the bead curtain against the table.

"The beer's nice and cool," the man said.

"It's lovely," the girl said.

Notice the unfolding here. Everything we read constitutes a beat of story time. There's nothing on the page that doesn't advance the story in time. There is no infolding and no interiority—the action never pauses to investigate the thoughts, perceptions, feelings, or memories of the characters. Now, the danger of purely unfolding a scene is that it will seem shallow or thin. But this one-scene story is neither. Why not? The most important factor is that for Hemingway, this style is not arbitrary. He must describe his characters' experience in this way because one of his deep convictions is the inadequacy of language to express inner pain. His characters are isolated, they are islands of lonely consciousness, and they occasionally shoot up inadequate flares to indicate their presence to others. So the lack of infolding doesn't mean there's nothing going on inside the characters—it means there *is*, and it's inaccessible, and that's part of his message. So how, without infolding, does he show us there's something here under the surface? How does he grip our attention with what is mostly a desultory conversation about cocktails?

Tension. There is tension between them. He is pressing something and she is resisting.

High stakes. What they are discussing—what they are also avoiding discussing—is morally and emotionally and spiritually troubling. It worries them and it worries us.

Rhythm. The statements that they make essentially match each other in terms of rhythm. There's a hypnotic quality to the development of the scene (this and then this, this and then this, and so on). In addition to these rhythmic exchanges, the scene is punctuated by the regular advancement and withdrawal of the waitress. *Do you want this drink? No. Here it is. Goodbye.*

Repetition. We hear the same language again and again. *Wasn't that bright. That was bright. Try this new drink. Try new drinks. Lovely hills. The beer is lovely. It's a simple operation. It's not an operation. It's the only thing that's made us unhappy. Then you think we'll be all right and happy. Afterward they were all so happy.* These repetitions emphasize the inadequacy of language, the little tinkling bell of language that tries in vain to render, or even to refer to, a symphony of hidden feeling.

Hemingway does one last thing here: in the entire story there is not a simile or metaphor except for the girl's description of the hills as white elephants. That is the sole moment in which someone uses a new level of language to stretch toward new meaning, the sole place in which unspoken or subconscious material pressing up against the tight grip of the abrupt sentences actually breaks through. And of course it's significant: the white elephants are a procession of unusual mythical creatures, famous for memory and for attachment; they are also a visual emblem of pregnancy—rounded white forms. So here a changeup in style—the use of image where there have been no images—also constitutes a major vibration in the taut construction of the scene. In this one place, the linguistic mode of a character is troubled by the unsaid and the unacknowledged.

Now let's leap to the first couple of pages of "Labor Day Dinner," by Alice Munro. It's scarcely a scene—it's the beginning of a scene—but look at what she does, and why.

> Just before six o'clock in the evening, George and Roberta and Angela and Eva get out of George's pickup truck—he traded his car for a pickup when he moved to the country—and walk

across Valerie's front yard, under the shade of two aloof and splendid elm trees that have been expensively preserved. Valerie says those trees cost her a trip to Europe. The grass underneath them has been kept green all summer, and is bordered by fiery dahlias. The house is of pale-red brick, and around the doors and windows there is a decorative outline of lighter-colored bricks, originally white. This style is often found in Grey County; perhaps it was a specialty of one of the early builders.

George is carrying the folding lawn chairs Valerie asked them to bring. Roberta is carrying a dessert, a raspberry bombe made from raspberries picked on their own farm—George's farm—earlier in the summer. She has packed it in ice cubes and wrapped it in dish towels, but she is eager to get it in the freezer. Angela and Eva carry bottles of wine. Angela and Eva are Roberta's daughters. It has been arranged between Roberta and her husband that they spend the summers with her and George and the school year in Halifax with him. Roberta's husband is in the Navy. Angela is seventeen, Eva is twelve.

These four people are costumed in a way that would suggest they were going to different dinner parties. George, who is a stocky, dark, barrel-chested man, with a daunting, professional look of self-assurance and impatience (he used to be a teacher), wears a clean T-shirt and nondescript pants. Roberta is wearing faded tan cotton pants and a loose raw-silk top of mud-brick color—a color that suits her dark hair and pale skin well enough when she is at her best, but she is not at her best today. When she made herself up in the bathroom, she thought her skin looked like a piece of waxed paper that had been crumpled into a tight ball and then smoothed out. She was momentarily pleased with her thinness and had planned to wear a slinky silver halter top she owns—a glamorous joke—but at the last minute she changed her mind. She is wearing dark glasses, and the reason is that she has taken to weeping spurts, never at the really bad times but in between; the spurts are as unbidden as sneezes.

You'll recognize the similarity to Woolf—the stretched scene. What we've got, in story versus discourse, is essentially one event—even a nonevent, a transition from one zone to another. What's it take, maybe sixty seconds, for four people to get out of a truck, pick up some items, and walk across a lawn? That little unit of action, however, is infolded tremendously. Munro simply says these people's names, gets them out of the truck and walking, and then takes each of them in midstep and patiently infolds, patiently enriches our vision of them. She wants that scene of them walking across the lawn, but she wants it to happen very slowly such that all this information can be attached to them, because these details are not whimsical. How Roberta sees herself, what her wardrobe is like, what kind of desserts she makes, who Valerie is, what sort of house she keeps, what the landscape is like, and the time of year and the climate, and George's barrel-chested competency and the ages of the girls—all these things are important to the story, which is about the passing of time, the forms of romance and family, and the inevitability of trouble and change.

Notice also that all this infolding allows Munro to proceed in an apparently indirect, apparently casual way to a central detail: Roberta is crying in spurts these days. (A hook with some power:

why is that lady crying?) Roberta's tears are crucial and yet are mentioned in a rich context of other important details. Whereas Hemingway moves relentlessly forward with action, speech, speech, action, Munro is more desultory and inclusive, creating a fabric of detail. Roberta's tears may be the silver thread drawing our attention, but the whole tapestry is as important as the individual characters and conflicts. The form is part of the meaning: the story concerns connections, threads, terminations, weaving; and the form of this scene is a tapestry.

Marilynne Robinson once said something in a workshop that was very useful to me (well, she said many things that were useful, as well as sublime, but this was especially good for me at the moment). She said that the reader is patient, that if you're showing something that is of significance and if your prose is good and if there are no missteps or squanderings of the reader's attention, then the reader will follow you anywhere. Because what's being related in the Munro section is so purposeful and specific, we can enjoy the pause in the action in which we hear about each of these people in a detailed way.

We have on the one hand Hemingway unfolding like crazy, and on the other hand Munro infolding like crazy; they're both brilliant. I'm offering that to you as a way of schematizing. If you start with these ideas, you'll have a greater grasp on that amorphous, imaginative thing that's happening inside you when you're trying to deploy or render a fictional world.

Let's look at one last scene, which does a couple of delightful things with scenic form. This is from *Hamlet*, act 1, scene 1. Obviously, this is drama, not fiction, so there can be no infolding. It can only be unfolding; everything that happens has to be played or said and therefore constitutes a note of story time. But there are a couple of things Shakespeare does in the opening of this greatest of plays that have implications for you in the making of your fictional scenes: he creates levels of actuality within the scene, and then moves between them, with startling effect.

> *Enter* Barnardo *and* Francisco, *two sentinels.*
>
> BARNARDO. Who's There?

Notice that at the moment the play begins, at those first words, something has already happened. The beginning of the scene is not the beginning. Somewhere out there in the time-space ether, before the commencement of the narrative and the commitment to scene, a noise has occurred and made itself known in the consciousness of a nervous man. The implication is that there is a world outside the world of the scene, where anything can happen or be happening, and which can affect the action we see in the scene. The scene continues:

> FRANCISCO. Nay, answer me. Stand and unfold yourself.
>
> BARNARDO. Long live the King!
>
> FRANCISCO. Barnardo?
>
> BARNARDO. He.
>
> FRANCISCO. You come most carefully upon your hour.
>
> BARNARDO. 'Tis now struck twelve. Get thee to bed, Francisco.
>
> FRANCISCO. For this relief much thanks.

The "Once upon a time" training in our brains prompts us to think that a narrative should begin at the beginning and that the tension and energy should increase until a turning point, when a balance is tipped. That's the conventional shape for a large narrative or a small one. But here we see that expectation flouted; we experience an entry into a moment of dramatic intensity that at once drops away. During the lull, the entrance of the skeptic Horatio provides occasion for Barnardo to tell his story again:

HORATIO. Tush, tush, twill' not appear.

BARNARDO. Sit down a while,
And let us once again assail your ears,
That are so fortified against our story,
What we two nights have seen.

So as Barnardo tells his story, we come to realize not only that the scene started one beat after the beginning of story time this evening but also that the story of this evening is happening after two other important evenings. We've been dropped onto a rapidly moving conveyor belt of narrative, and it's disorienting and thrilling.

HORATIO. Well, sit we down,
And let us hear Barnardo speak of this.

BARNARDO. Last night of all,
When yond same star that's westward from the pole
Had made his course t'illume that part of heaven
Where it now burns, Marcellus and myself,
The bell then beating one—

As Horatio does, we sit down and listen to a story within a story (as there later will be a play within the play). We sit still with Horatio, listening to and imagining what is being described. We are taken out of the hypothetical reality of the castle roof tonight in order to go to another level, to inhabit the hypothetical reality of the castle roof last night. Surely nothing is going to happen in the physical world of this scene, right?

BARNARDO. Last night of all,
When yond same star that's westward from the pole
Had made his course t'illume that part of heaven
Where it now burns, Marcellus and myself,
The bell then beating one—

Enter Ghost

MARCELLUS. Peace, break thee off; look, where it comes again!

Just as Barnardo is on the point of saying, "Last night this ghost turned up," the actual appearance of the ghost makes us jump out of the told story into the present story of the scene itself. So even within a scene there are various levels of narrative actuality. You can be moving forward unfolding story, or you can be infolding character and other material, but you can also structure the scene with layers of narrative: story within story, play within play.

Imagine a scene in which a man tells his coworker about a vacation he took. During the vacation, he went to an art gallery and he saw a painting. In the painting he saw a lonely little pond in the woods. As he looked at the lonely little pond in the painting, he imagined a mermaid who lived in the pond. Then he fell in love with the mermaid.

Having established all those layers, the writer can make something happen on any of them: the love the man has for the mermaid, the mermaid in the pond, the lonely little pond in the woods, the surface of the painting, the vacation, or the storytelling about the vacation. There is a dimensionality you can create by going below the surface of your own narrative. The classic way is the story within the story, but writers are always at liberty to evoke and use other media within their fictions: paintings, songs, documents. All these media have narrative and symbolic value, and they are all ways to layer the actuality in scenes.

A tremendous contemporary example is the novella *Ordinary Love*, by Jane Smiley, in which a woman and her adult children, who have gathered for the first time in a long time, tell each other stories. The woman hears the tale of a terrifying event in her children's lives that she'd never before known about. The told story engenders the reorganizing of this woman's sense of her family and is the crux of the novella. In the "real world" of the scene, the characters don't do much except sit around and drink beer and yet the world of the characters has undergone a tremendous shift. .

I'll end with an observation I heard made by the short-fiction writer Deborah Eisenberg: You can do anything you want to do, as long as you can do it. If you can pull it off, you can do anything. If you can make it work, you can do anything you want. The scene, like fiction itself, is superbly elastic.

LE MOT INCORRECT

JIM KRUSOE

I

A FEW WEEKS ago, on a Tuesday afternoon I think, but possibly not, the phone rang. I answered it to hear a friend of mine tell me with maybe a little too much glee in his voice that he had just figured out why it had taken me so long—well into my fifties—to publish fiction. "For most people," my friend said, "all they have to do is to choose one word out of the maybe five or ten or twenty that are available in order to get the one that is exactly right. That's because they are trying for that old Flaubertian idea of 'le mot juste.' But you, Jim, in your efforts to select not the correct but the *incorrect* word, how many more possibilities do you have to choose from?"

Cradling the phone between my ear and my shoulder, I stood at the sink, stripping off pieces of the—what do you call it?— *rind* from broccoli stalks, a trick I learned from a French restaurant in, of all places, Baja California, an establishment that had the miraculous policy of charging the same price for every meal, whether it was a waffle or a steak. I had taken the trip with my former wife as one last attempt to make a failing marriage work. (It didn't.) I tried to interject that choosing the right word probably wasn't as simple as he, my friend, was making it sound, and we shouldn't disrespect writers who strive along those lines. My friend, however, was just getting started, because that's the kind of person he is: he gets excited by ideas, and most of all he takes pleasure, as well he should, in his own.

"Well maybe," my friend said with doubt in his voice. "But think about it. For most writers, if they want to mention someone's elbow, for example, they have the words *joint*, or *connection*, or *angle*, or *bend*, or even *hairpin curve*: not so many choices, really, when you think about it. You, however, in your pioneering efforts, Jim, have not only all of those words that I've just mentioned but also *knee*, and *hopscotch*, and *window*, plus nearly everything else. And then," he paused significantly, "after you have finally chosen that word, you have to choose the word that comes after that, and then the word after that."

I could hear him thinking on the other end of the phone as the vast implications of what he'd just said began to dawn on him. I sliced the peeled stalks and put them in a steamer, then moved the pot over to the stove and lit a burner. "Why," my friend gasped, "it's a miracle that you ever even finished one story, let alone a book, considering everything. You don't know any foreign languages, do you?"

"No," I said.

"Thank God," he said.

I laughed modestly. "But it's not quite so hard as you make it out to be. Fortunately, there are rules to help a person along, just as there are for other things in life that initially seem puzzling, even though, as elsewhere, naturally, those rules are constantly being changed, challenged, or turn out to be of no use whatsoever."

Then the conversation shifted to other things, the broccoli stalks cooked, and it was only a couple days later that I began to think again about the idea of "le mot incorrect." What more, I wondered—as I applied my elbow to hurl the paper airplane of that subject into the brisk breeze coming in through an open window only a hairpin turn away—might be said about the matter?

II

BUT BEFORE WE go further, let's take a small step backward.

That is, let me begin by playing devil's advocate and discuss for a moment how comforting and attractive the concept of "the right word" truly is. Wasn't it Robert Browning, for example, who wrote, in a poem I never finished reading, "God's in his Heaven—/ All's right with the world!"? Or, to quote John Wayne in *Red River* as he spoke to Montgomery Clift while they were attempting to drive hundreds of cattle—cattle, my father used to point out to me, with the air of a connoisseur, that were all different, because whereas in a lesser movie the director would simply rent a dozen or so cattle and run the same weary steers by the cameras over and over to create the impression of a herd, one of the reasons *Red River* is a classic is because Howard Hawks took the trouble to use hundreds, maybe even thousands of cattle, and run them by the camera only once, all those dozens and dozens of cows like "mots incorrect," it now occurs to me—what John Wayne said was, "Be sure you're right, then go ahead." Or as Allen Ginsberg used to say years later, curiously echoing the Duke, "First thought, best thought."

So I will make no bones about it: I understand the great magnetism of "le mot juste" is that it allows a writer to conjure up a romantic picture of him or herself, the captain of his or her craft, a steady hand on the tiller, moving relentlessly forward over the waves of deep, clear thought, pausing, thinking, checking the depths, studying the charts, choosing, correcting course, until at last the final destination is reached, the cargo is unloaded, and the crew, except for an unlucky few who must remain onboard to guard the ship, is on shore leave. Only then will this writer/captain walk over to the ship's log, pick it up, make a correction here or an erasure there, perhaps have a glass of sherry, and then send the log off to be published. Nor is this completely impossible. I actually know one writer (albeit, the only one) who enacted what I'm sure is every author's dream: upon receiving his proofread manuscript with dozens of niggling changes from the publisher, he simply wrote "STET" on the cover page and sent it back.

Not me, however. For me and most of the writers I know, the sea is not quite so deep or clear or blue, but more like a formerly clear creek rendered nearly opaque by the crossing of hundreds, if not thousands, of cattle, and the possibility of being able to see the bottom, let alone to spot the exact word that one needs lying there and upon finding it, to bring it back to the surface, seems unlikely. My own experience, more desperate than most,

I'll admit, is that before I send a book to the publisher it's been through at least fifteen drafts; the manuscript has been shown to at least a dozen people and even read aloud to restless and indifferent crowds, all resulting in sometimes major changes before an actual editor ever gets to see it and cringe. So when, exactly, does this process start being exact?

Maybe never. You show me a word or a sentence, and I'll show you things to be said for it and against it, and in the end I won't be sure, only *pretty* sure, that I'm right, and if not "right," at least I'm sure that I can't do any better. At that moment.

III

So IF YOU are still with me, let's take yet one more step backward, this time down the mud-tracked corridors of high school until we are both standing in the familiar footprints of tenth-grade logic, which divides reason into two parts: deductive and inductive. With deductive reasoning you start from the top and work your way down to discover a principle that applies to everything and will always apply, because the whole is larger than the sum of its parts. That's exactly the type of logic I most fervently longed and wished for as a lonely teenager, alone in my lonely room, unhappy and awkward, because it was clear to me that if my future boiled down to only my visible parts, I didn't stand a chance. With inductive reasoning, on the other hand, you start with the parts and try to come up with an explanation of how they work: what they have in common. This means, naturally, that every time a new example comes into view, the generalization you have just made is threatened, and the parts might overwhelm the whole. And how scornful I used to be, as a lonely teen, of *that* process.

Deductive reasoning is the basis for the French legal system, the Napoleonic Code, with one judge and no jury. It's probably no coincidence that much of French literature seems to be about ideas, and those characters who first pop into my head when I think of French novels, Candide and Meursault, are in fact both embodiments of ideas.

Nor is it a coincidence that that great French maker of *real* characters, Proust, famously used Charles Dickens as his model; it's often been observed that the English novel springs not from ideas but from characters. This means that though there may be ideas inherent in the work, we are led to them through the actions of the characters, and usually we form our ideas only after the smoke has cleared. The ideas come from the bottom up, and as a result a "well-drawn" character exhibits all sorts of contradictions. Another way of putting it (maybe mine, but I no longer remember) is that a character is a person who gets into trouble.

The attraction of the deductive method of writing is the feeling of authority it produces, and certainly if one considers the critical literature of the past fifty years, a good bit of the most authoritative—Barthes, Derrida, and Lacan—happen to be French in origin. The advantages of inductive reasoning include innovation, or at least flexibility, and the possibility of accidental discovery. In a way it's humorous that the great French school of experimentation, the Oulipo workshop, out of which came Italo Calvino, and Georges Perec, and Raymond Queneau, and the American (!) Harry Matthews, was dedicated to prescribed patterns of improvisation, to exact formulas for astonishment.

IV

FRANK O'HARA ONCE quoted Franz Kline as saying, "To be right is the most terrific personal state that nobody is interested in." This same interview, by the way, which appears in *Art Chronicles*, includes one of my favorite quotes of all time, which says that a Bohemian artist is "someone who could live where animals would die," reminding me of a wedding reception a fellow poet threw for himself and sweetly invited me to attend back in the seventies in Venice, California. It was outdoors, and the bride, a heroin addict, sat near their trailer on one of those metal lawn chairs with a pattern of holes drilled in the back and stared at a point nowhere on this planet as she worked through a stack of *Vogue* magazines, distractedly covering every page with scribbles from a worn-down pink crayon. "She's an artistic genius," the groom whispered to me while he followed an extension cord he had run from his neighbor's house to an electric fry pan in the vacant lot where the reception was taking place. He poked the entrée, chicken backs in catsup, with a stick. "They're almost ready," he confided. The bride, as they say, looked *radiant*. And let me observe here that it may have been a part of the seventies, or just a part of being young, but who was to say back then that she *couldn't* have been a genius, that in an art world where arranging strips of lumber on a floor was acclaimed, or painting a canvas a single color got a museum show, she wasn't as good as any other, maybe better? In the end I lost touch with my friend the poet, and whatever happened to his wife and that stack of *Vogue* magazines turned into art, I never learned.

What am I trying to say here? Only that the advantages of "les mots incorrect" should be self-evident: wrong words help us stray off the path, not by producing a new path, but by throwing us into the thicket, and if it's too dark to see, then it's up to us to plug in that fry pan, that "mot incorrect," and use the little glowing red light set in the handle that tells us when the desired temperature has been reached to find a way out. Like black holes, which suck everything into them, "mots incorrect" come in all sizes: words, metaphors, sentences, paragraphs, even chapters. When I'm stuck in a story or in a novel I usually think: "What the hell? Between a dull book and no book at all, there's not much of a difference. You're going nowhere, so getting lost can only help." One of the nice things about writing is that unlike in life—the life of my poet friend, for example—if things get too scary, we can always cross them out and return to the last place we knew we were making sense. What hidden bolus of middle-class convention it was that caused my friend to throw a wedding reception in the first place I will never know. For that matter, what made me think a vacation in Mexico would save my marriage?

Being right is what life is (wrongly) supposed to be about: having the right taste, doing the right thing. But in writing, correctness not only stops the conversation between the writer and the reader, it also stops it between the writer and her or himself. To have no questions is to cease to explore. A poor piece with all the right words has nowhere to turn. Wrong words, however, put us into a different relationship with our sentences and our work. They open up a discussion with the reader that involves language, metaphor, and plot. The reader gets to ask, just as the writer asks, where the hell is this going anyway? Is it working for me? Why or why not? If, like me, you are lazy, "le mot incorrect" will throw you into the murky pool of uncertainty and get you paddling, or at least bobbing.

There's a story that I'm fond of telling, though I can't even remember where I first heard it. A German scholar was on a train in Japan and the only other person in his compartment was a Zen monk. It was a hot day, and the scholar was just beginning to doze in the airless carriage of the train when he heard the monk sitting across from him say in English, "I trust you are having an enjoyable visit to Japan."

The German roused himself and replied that he was, and after exchanging a few pleasantries he learned that the monk was from a monastery, the name of which the scholar recognized.

The monk asked if he would care for a drink of cold tea. The German said that he would, and from beneath his seat the monk produced a container made of unglazed clay, sweating slightly, and partially wrapped in straw. The monk poured two cups of tea and handed one to the German, who sipped it. The tea was surprisingly bitter and tasted somewhat of dirt.

The scholar emptied his cup and lowered it. "I have heard" he said, "that in your monastery you have a monk who, though blind, can aim his arrow so he hits the bull's-eye a hundred times in a row."

"Oh him," the Zen monk said, finishing his tea. "Yes, he's there. But if you want to know the truth there's another monk that we are all far more impressed by." Then the monk made a gesture to inquire if the scholar would like more tea.

The German shook his head no. He was astounded. "How can this be?" he said. "What can this second man do that the first one can't?"

The Zen monk smiled. He put the two cups back in his pack and returned the container of tea to beneath his seat. "You should know that this second man is also blind and an archer," he said. "But though he has been aiming at the target for his entire life, shooting hundreds of arrows each day, he has never managed to hit the mark even once."

I don't know if this is true, but Alice Fulton once told a group I was in about studying with the poet A. R. Ammons. What Ammons would do as a teacher, Fulton said, was that upon finding the one part, or line, or phrase of a poem that didn't seem to work, instead of suggesting that the student take it out, he would say, "Look at this. Now this is interesting. What did you mean by this?" Meaning, of course, that everything we do is often already too well known to us. It's in our so-called mistakes that we have the hope of finding a new meaning. Or, to quote Francis Bacon in regard to his method of painting: it's "accident engendering accident."

And speaking of Zen, there's a small Zen poem in a lovely book, *The Japanese Chronicles*, by a lovely writer, Nicolas Bouvier.

> Stop worrying
> And follow the flow
> If your thoughts are connected
> They lose their freshness
>
> —Seng-T'san

V

HERE, THEN, ARE a few suggestions, possibly incorrect, that I will offer up in an effort to help you to get lost.

Regarding words
1. If you can't think of the exact wrong word, try a wrong-phrase, or even a couple wrong sentences.
2. Antonyms are sometimes better than synonyms. If you must use a thesaurus, go to the list of opposite meanings.
3. Sometimes alliteration produces interesting results. The writer David Mura once said that when he can't think of a word, or has a choice between two words, he usually chooses one that starts with the same letter as the word next to it.

Regarding similes and metaphors
1. Instead of using a simile or metaphor that illuminates the object being described, try one that completely overwhelms the object both in its size and by the fact that it's more interesting. Someone once sent me one of those lists that circulate on the Internet—this one was of similes used by high school students (I believe they were referred to as "actual high school students") that illustrate exactly what I'm describing: "He spoke with the wisdom that can only come from experience, like a guy who went blind because he looked at a solar eclipse without one of those boxes with a pinhole in it and now goes around the country speaking about the dangers of looking at a solar eclipse without one of those boxes with a

pinhole in it." "From the attic came an unearthly howl. The whole scene had an eerie surreal quality, like when you're on vacation in another city and *Jeopardy* comes on at 7 PM instead of 7:30."

2. Instead of saying what it's like, try saying what it's not like: an anti-metaphor or an anti-simile. Again, here is a selection from an actual high school student: "The little boat gently drifted across the pond exactly the way a bowling ball wouldn't."

Regarding sentences

1. I love sentences that go on talking long after they have finished what they started out saying. In that way they can get hopelessly lost, or contradict, or even incriminate the idea that they began with. For example, much of Henry James's style is based on wonderfully long sentences whose job it often is to qualify and retract whatever statement the sentence began with.

2. There is always possibility to be found in writing a sentence that says what you don't know, rather than what you do know.

Regarding paragraphs

1. Paragraphs aren't the time for flashbacks; whole chapters work much better. But a paragraph in a story is a wonderful chance to put in a list, or an "objective" note of scientific or historical interest.

2. You can add a paragraph to the middle of a story where someone writes or reads a letter, or confesses something.

This sometimes has the effect of opening a window on the narrative and letting in some air.

Regarding chapters
1. If you must use a flashback, this is where it belongs, in a whole luxurious chapter all to itself.
2. Use a chapter to change the setting of the action.
3. Use a chapter to change the time of the action.
4. Use a chapter to change (although I'm very wary about this one) the point of view.

VI

FINALLY, I HAVE a confession to make: one of the very few things I find appalling about teaching (but it's also true in other walks of life) is the phenomenon of people—often students—who feel they are qualified to pass the most disdainful sort of judgment on any writer, no matter how great, living or dead, whose work happens to fall under their scrutiny. The result is—and I admit to having done this myself a time or two—scary dismissals of those whose boots, as they say, I am not fit to clean. (And if you think it's bad in graduate school, I'm here to let you know it's even worse among undergraduates, who, for some reason I can't understand, feel entitled not only to criticize but also to assume a first-name basis with the objects of their derision: "I just think Leo takes too long getting started in *Anna Karenina*" or "I couldn't get into all that Catholic stuff of Flannery's.")

So I would like to go back for a moment to the very great writer Gustave—Flaubert, that is—whose coinage of "le mot juste" began this whole digression, and to note that it was quite by accident that I left Emma Bovary out of the list of major idea-driven characters in French novels, but that may well be because she does not feel in the least driven by ideas, but by empathy and, of course, love.

And I have yet one more confession to make. When I began to think about this idea of "le mot juste," it had been thirty years since I had actually read *Madame Bovary*; in other words, I had never read it as a writer, only as a consumer, and my recollections, other than "what happened," were pretty dim. So you can imagine my surprise on my second time around as I watched the cruise missile of the perfect narrative take aim straight at the title, at Madame Bovary, and then proceed not to hit Madame Bovary at all, but her husband-to-be, Charles, and then not even him as an adult, but as a young boy, and then not even hit the young boy, but his hat, which Flaubert famously describes for a whole paragraph as early as the second page. And then, unbelievably, the missile still manages not to hit the title character herself but follows Charles through an indifferent college career and a first unhappy marriage to an entirely different Madame Bovary. Madame Bovary No. 1 keels over while hanging some washing, and it's not until page fourteen of the Penguin English edition that we see Madame Bovary No. 2, Emma, at eighteen years old, licking the blood from her fingers where she has pricked them sewing a strap for her father's broken leg. And most unbelievably of all, the narrator of all this is not the title character, or Charles

Bovary (who will later cause a man's leg to be amputated by "fixing" it), or even the author, but an unnamed someone who claims to have been a schoolmate of Charles's.

So not only am I not certain that what I mean by "le mot juste" is the same as what Flaubert himself meant, I'm not sure what others mean either. My own ideas about "the correct way to write" seem at best like the answer you give the clerk at the motel when he asks you if you are married to the man or woman you've just walked in with: "Sure, if we need to be."

Therefore those who elevate the standard of the perfect word should take note. No one who looks at a page of *A Sentimental Education* in Flaubert's own hand can possibly fail to recognize it was written by a person who allowed himself to become deeply lost in one thicket or another. Nor can anyone read *Salambo*, the novel that followed *Madame Bovary*, and believe that choosing "le mot juste" will save a writer from missteps. Even Flaubert's most dedicated disciples when defending that book are more or less reduced to "You had to have been there."

And most tellingly, the author who created *Madame Bovary*, which many have called the first realistic novel, for his final work created what is perhaps one of the masterpieces of "le mot incorrect," *Bouvard and Pécuchet*, the near-plotless narrative of two friends who retire to the country to create, in the manner of Diderot, an encyclopedia of human knowledge. In this book, to quote Jorge Luis Borges, who is paraphrasing another critic, Flaubert "dreamed of an epic of human idiocy." Flaubert, Borges says, makes the two title characters "read an entire library *so that they will not understand it* . . . in order to come up with the reactions of his two imbeciles, [Flaubert] read one thousand five hundred treatises on agronomy, pedagogy, medicine, physics, metaphysics, etc., in the aim of not understanding them."

Bouvard and Pécuchet took six years to write and in fact was published before it was complete. And while Remy de Gourmont saw the book (again, according to Borges) as "the principal work of French literature, and almost of literature itself," Borges himself reads the book as a Swiftian parable buttressed by Flaubert's lifelong disdain for the trappings of human intellect: the reduction of all human yearning to the "ridiculous and insignificant."

But there is, of course, another interpretation. Like the Sufi parables, stories that have been handed down more or less intact from generation to generation (just as Flaubert buried his own parable about the persistence of hope and purity inside the adultery of a middle-class woman), perhaps we may also dare to assume that the surest way to preserve the truest knowledge of the world is to hide it in the great thicket of misinformation, stupidity, accident, and incorrectness that still endures and which, as Faulkner writes, shall almost certainly prevail.

SHAKESPEARE FOR WRITERS
Sixteen Lessons

MARGOT LIVESEY

It would not be entirely accurate to claim that Shakespeare is a writer with whom I have a lifelong acquaintance, though perhaps my mother attended a production of *Twelfth Night* or *Hamlet* when I was in utero. Certainly I think it likely that my parents read aloud to me from Lamb's *Tales from Shakespeare*; I can still picture the mild blue cover of the book. And my father, at trying moments, frequently quoted Lear's complaint: "Sharper than a serpent's tooth it is to have a thankless child." My own independent relationship with Shakespeare began when I was nine, the year I started elocution lessons. These were held in the drawing room of the private school I attended at that time. I remember lying on the carpeted floor, staring up at the walls, which were paneled in yellow fabric, and practicing breathing from the diaphragm. Then I was allowed to stand up and recite Puck's speech from *A Midsummer Night's Dream*:

Through the forest have I gone,
But Athenian found I none
On whose eyes I might approve
This flower's force in stirring love.

Later that year I was cast as Jessica, Shylock's daughter, in *The Merchant of Venice*. I gazed raptly at Lorenzo, played by another nine-year-old girl, while he declaimed:

How sweet the moonlight sleeps upon this bank!
Here will we sit and let the sounds of music
Creep in our ears: soft stillness and the night
Become the touches of sweet harmony.
Sit, Jessica. Look how the floor of heaven
Is thick inlaid with patens of bright gold:
There's not the smallest orb which thou behold'st
But in his motion like an angel sings,
Still quiring to the young-eyed cherubins;
Such harmony is in immortal souls;
But whilst this muddy vesture of decay
Doth grossly close it in, we cannot hear it.

And what does Jessica say in response to these beautiful words? "I am never merry when I hear sweet music." No wonder I envied my suitor and learned his lines as well as my own.

From then on I studied several plays a year. I was particularly enthralled by *Macbeth*, which is set in Scotland. My parents and I regularly drove past Birnam Wood on our way to visit my aunt, and I always thought about the witches' promise to

Macbeth—that he's safe until Birnam Wood comes to Dunsinane Hill—and how cleverly the meaning of that promise is subverted by having the soldiers carry broken-off branches as camouflage. On my most recent visit to Scotland I noticed that the town of Birnam now advertises something called The Macbeth Experience. Sadly, I have not yet had a chance to investigate this.

In spite of this long acquaintance, however, I was relatively slow to consider what I could learn as a writer from our great forebear. Iris Murdoch famously claimed to have borrowed all her plots from Shakespeare. And of course other writers, such as Jane Smiley, Tom Stoppard, and John Updike, have reimagined, or extended, his work. Such borrowings would surely have gratified the playwright, who famously borrowed many of his own great plots, and I do want to address that aspect of his work, but what I mostly want to focus on are issues of craft and what writers can learn from his example. To that end I am ignoring a mountain of criticism and scholarship, ranging from the sublimely eloquent and brilliantly argued to the specious and dull.

Shakespeare was lucky to live and work during a comparatively peaceful period in English history when theater flourished. Thirty-six plays are, more or less, attributed to him, along with several long poems and, of course, the beloved sonnets. Of the plays, perhaps half are performed and read frequently. Looking at several of those that aren't is instructive. While there are wonderful moments, gorgeous turns of phrase, I also find Shakespeare making poor use of two of his favorite devices: mistaken identity and/or disguise and the (potentially incredibly annoying) feigned death. It is reassuring to know that he could be less than great and that it sometimes took him several attempts to find the right form for the material. We seldom approach a piece of work planning for it to be a failure, but in hindsight we do sometimes realize that we needed to write *Henry VI* in order to learn how to write *Henry IV*. (The history plays were not written chronologically.)

Considering Shakespeare's work as a whole also reminds us that almost all writers are drawn back, unconsciously, to their own essential—one might say primal—patterns. Young writers, I think, often feel they can repeat themselves because no one is paying attention, but if we want to keep going, we have to become increasingly vigilant about recognizing what we've already accomplished and turning a deaf ear to those sirens that would lure us back onto the rocks of repetition.

In this essay I'll revisit four of the best known plays and discuss some of what they can teach us. First a comedy: *A Midsummer Night's Dream*, written in the winter of 1595. Second a history play: *Henry IV, Part 1*, probably written in 1596–97. Third, what I would call a tragicomedy: *The Merchant of Venice*, which was initially performed in the summer of 1598. And lastly *King Lear*, first performed as a cheery Christmas celebration on December 26, 1605.

Let me provide a tediously brief description of each play. *A Midsummer Night's Dream* is often regarded as Shakespeare's first mature play and is certainly one of his best loved and most frequently performed. Mendelssohn wrote occasional music for it, Benjamin Britten wrote an exquisite opera, and even as I write countless productions are being rehearsed in theaters, school gymnasiums, and parks. Although the play owes a debt to Ovid's *Metamorphoses*, which, with its captivating stories of violence and transformation, was an Elizabethan best-seller, it is one of the few plays in which Shakespeare seems to have largely invented the plot, and the result is both intricate and simple. Hermia wants to marry Lysander rather than her father's choice of Demetrius, who is the beloved of Hermia's best friend, Helena. The four well-nigh indistinguishable lovers flee the court of Theseus to enter a wood near Athens, where they get caught up in the feud between the fairy king and queen, as do a group of Athenian workmen who are rehearsing their own play. Magic ensues, and eventually the lovers emerge from the woods, successfully reconfigured.

The Merchant of Venice is another much-beloved and much-performed play. Like *A Midsummer Night's Dream*, it is set in a European country that we have no reason to think either the author or his original audience knew much about, and it involves romantic love, but in this case Shakespeare combined familiar plots from at least two sources—the casket plot and the flesh-for-money plot—to a more solemn end. He would also surely have been aware of several recent plays with Jewish characters, including Christopher Marlowe's *The Jew of Malta*. The casket plot is driven by Bassanio, who, wellborn but poor, wants to woo the wealthy Portia. According to her father's will she must marry the man who chooses the casket—gold, silver, or lead—that contains her portrait. The wrong choice carries significant penalties. Bassanio's friend Antonio, a wealthy merchant whose fortune is presently bound up in various ships, agrees to finance his wooing by borrowing money from Shylock and signs a deed that he will forfeit a pound of flesh if he can't pay his debt. Bassanio's wooing prospers, Antonio's ships flounder, and the two plots converge in one of our earliest courtroom dramas.

Reimagining English history proved fruitful territory for Shakespeare, especially during the first half of his career. As I've mentioned, he did not approach this task chronologically. He had already written the Henry VI trilogy and *Richard III* and *II* before he turned back to the charismatic Henry V, who, against huge odds, won the Battle of Agincourt. *Henry IV, Part 1*, shows the young Prince Hal, the future Henry V, emerging from the pubs and brothels of London to become a worthy heir. Like *A Midsummer Night's Dream*, the play is set between two worlds: the world of drink and disorder where the stout, witty, pragmatic Falstaff is king and the world of political ambition and unrest where Henry IV, Hal's father, is struggling to hold on to his power. The question is will the dissolute prince rise to these challenges and overcome the ambitious, accomplished, and—in the production I recently saw in London—mouthwateringly handsome Hotspur?

King Lear is also set in England against a background of political unrest. I'd feel foolish summarizing this play, so I'll just say it concerns two fathers each deceived in his children, mistaking good for bad and bad for good, who suffer terrible consequences as a result of their mistakes.

You might rightly point out that I've already contravened one of the major lessons of these four plays, which is "Don't waste time." Don't bother with prologues, don't hold back the good stuff, just plunge your audience into an interesting situation and assume that they'll follow you. This seems so obvious as to be scarcely worth mentioning, but when I looked again at the opening scenes of each of these plays, I found that over and above being interesting they are also full of tension, and that the tension, like the interest, derives not, as is sometimes the case in contemporary work, from the voice but from the situation. Hermia's father is determined she will marry Demetrius, and Hermia is determined she will marry Lysander. Lear is determined to divide his kingdom according to his daughters' rhetoric, and Cordelia refuses to play the game. Henry IV is faced with rebellion, and his son is too busy partying with Falstaff to help. Bassanio, despite lack of funds and the risks of choosing the wrong casket, insists on pursuing Portia.

Also striking, if one reads these openings in the context of contemporary fiction, is that they begin in the present. No casting forward to the death of the protagonist three months hence, no remembering the night the heroine came home a decade earlier to find her mother burning her father's tap shoes. Shakespeare doesn't use flashbacks, and his characters are more likely to philosophize than to remember. The interesting and dramatic openings are happening right now and propel us into the future, not the past. What would he have made of Harold Pinter's play *Betrayal*, in which, from the opening scene, we go steadily back into past events? Or Martin Amis's novel *Time's Arrow*? I'm not arguing against this device—an arresting event followed by a leap backward or forward—only suggesting that perhaps writers favor it a little too much.

Another lesson to be garnered from these openings has to do with plausibility. The poet Coleridge complained that the beginning of *King Lear*—the elderly king dividing his kingdom among his three daughters and going on to banish Cordelia and his loyal servant Kent—was grossly improbable. And one might say the same of the very peculiar business arrangement between Antonio and Shylock. How many of us borrowing money would consent to sign away a pound of flesh as collateral? And why go to a money lender one has frequently slighted, as is the case with Antonio and Shylock? In *A Midsummer Night's Dream*, we must negotiate our way past at least two unlikely events. First we have to believe that Helena, on hearing about Hermia's proposed elopement, would, rather than rejoicing that her rival is out of the picture, betray the plan to Demetrius in the hope of winning his favor. And then there is the quarrel between Oberon and Titania—a quarrel so severe, Titania tells us that the entire world is in disarray:

> The ox hath therefore stretch'd his yoke in vain,
> The plowman lost his sweat, and the green corn
> Hath rotted ere his youth attain'd a beard;
> The fold stands empty in the drowned field.

The moon is pale with anger, and the seasons themselves have changed their wonted livery. The ostensible cause of all this is a changeling boy. Titania claims she won't give him up because of her love for his dead mother. Oberon doesn't even attempt an explanation, though we suspect that his orneriness is fueled by a longing to annoy his wife, perhaps because of jealousy over their mutual affairs. But these improbable events happen so early on, are so much a given of the play, that we aren't in a position to question them. And if we did, Titania's gorgeous speech of nearly forty lines describing not the origins but the escalating effects of the quarrel would surely dissuade us from such unprofitable speculations. Poetry conquers all.

However implausible Shakespeare is in his opening scenes, once he has established the rules of the world he's creating—and he almost always is creating a world markedly different than the one his audience left on entering the theater—he is usually at some pains to keep them. Though we may quibble, mildly, over the number of convenient letters, storms, and resurrections, we appreciate his desire to keep faith with us.

I'd also argue that plausibility in art is not always devoutly to be wished for. Certain gestures that don't make actual sense make poetic sense. In Caryl Churchill's play *Top Girls*, a group of famous women from several centuries sit down to dinner in a thoroughly satisfying way. In Michael Faber's novel *Under the Skin*, we empathize with the main character, Isserley, for many pages before realizing that she is an animal, and that she is picking up human hitchhikers for food. When one stops to think about *King Lear*, it is very odd that Cordelia's devoted husband leaves her alone in England to defeat her sisters' armies. But we don't stop to think, in part because the play is rushing headlong at this point and in part because we recognize intuitively that Lear and Cordelia, who have been separated by their mutual stubbornness in act 1, must now meet alone, without encumbrances, to work out their tragic reconciliation. Similarly, we tend not to question why Portia, with no legal experience, insists on disguising herself as a lawyer and arguing Antonio's case against Shylock. Poetically, it makes sense that she and Shylock must confront each other and that the verbal cunning her father has used on her suitors is now employed by her to save her husband's friend.

One of the dictums haunting fiction writers, and maybe poets and dramatists too, is Hemingway's remark that the writer can leave out anything so long as he or she knows what it is. To my mind this claim, in its most sweeping form, is indefensible. Imagine *The Old Man and the Sea* without the fish, say, or Michael Cunningham's *The Hours* without the party, or Francine Prose's *Blue Angel* without the impossibly precocious student. Of course this isn't what Hemingway meant; he exaggerated to remind us of the artifice of realism and the necessity of selection. One factor in Shakespeare's enduring greatness is his gift for omission. While he labors to make his plots work in a nuts-and-bolts fashion—here's how Portia got to the courtroom, here's how Gloucester died offstage so as not to detract from Lear and Cordelia—he does omit a good deal. Typically, he omits journeys unless they make a difference. And frequently he omits the psychological explanations so beloved of contemporary writers.

Production after production of *The Merchant of Venice* struggles to make sense of Antonio's melancholy and of his huge, and not sufficiently requited, affection for Bassanio. The current popular solution is to make Antonio gay, but for most of the play's history, audiences seemed happy to believe in profound, asexual male friendship of a kind they recognized from the Greeks and from various Elizabethan romances. The British writer Ford Madox Ford said that the novelist should first interest the reader, then explain. While Shakespeare does an admirable job of following the first half of this advice, he often, flagrantly, neglects the second. In *King Lear* we are given no insight into why Cordelia is so closemouthed. In *A Midsummer Night's Dream* the drug-induced affections of the lovers seem, in depth and passion, very similar to their real feelings. Motivation is often left out and provided, or not, by the actors and, of course, by the readers and viewers.

While I'm on this topic, let me digress for a moment to reflect on audiences and what they do for a text. In *Aspects of the Novel*, E. M. Forster famously claims that if you say the king dies and then the queen dies you don't have a plot, but if you say the queen dies because of grief you do. I would argue, however, that readers nowadays tend to be very good at filling in the "because" and that when two events are juxtaposed readers almost invariably link them. Even when the writer is doing her or his best to thwart them—insisting, for example, that a character's dream is meaningless—readers tend to supply a connection.

As for Shakespeare, even when he does explain, he often undercuts or complicates the explanation. In *Lear*, Gloucester argues that Edmund's bad behavior is due to his illegitimacy, and although we might agree that having a father who's constantly remarking on this must be trying, this theory is called into question by the equally bad behavior of Lear's legitimate daughters. Shakespeare is determined not to allow us to choose either nature or nurture as the key to character. "In sooth," says Antonio at the beginning of *The Merchant of Venice*, "I know not why I am so sad."

Other explanations seem frankly unconvincing from the start. When Prince Hal claims that he is carousing with Falstaff so that as a prodigal son he will shine more brightly when he returns to the fold, we are, I think, rightly skeptical. (Many members of the current British royal family, however, do seem to have taken this speech to heart.)

Of course, we can argue that Shakespeare was writing for performance, and anyone who has had the good fortune to see several different productions of the same play knows the profound difference that actors, directors, and designers can make. What he so felicitously leaves out, they fill in. It is also worth pointing out that we live in a more self-conscious age; readers and writers alike are committed to Freud's sofa. So please understand I'm not saying, "Don't explain." How much less moving Tim O'Brien's story "The Things They Carried" would be if we didn't discover that Lieutenant Jimmy Cross's fatal inattention is due to his hopeless romantic daydreams. But I think there is a useful reminder in Shakespeare about the limits of explanation. Perhaps to the much-qualified dictum "Show, don't tell," we need to add another qualified admonition: "Actions speak as loudly as explanations and don't always need to be explained." In Flannery O'Connor's "Good Country People," when the Bible salesman steals Hulga's wooden leg, we neither need nor want to be told why.

As I remarked earlier, Shakespeare borrowed the vast majority of his plots. In our age borrowing is a more complicated matter, and the boundary between homage and plagiarism, as David Leavitt and D. M. Thomas have discovered, is sometimes confusingly vague. I'm not sure that a general pronouncement on the subject is possible except to say be careful from whom you borrow and why, but four aspects of Shakespeare's modus operandi are surely worth noting: He didn't conceal his borrowing but typically used the same names, as in *King Lear*—a play also called *King Lear* had appeared in London a few years earlier. He often combined material from several sources, as in *Lear* and *The Merchant of Venice*. He wasn't afraid to make changes—in the source that he probably used for the casket story, Portia is a widow. Lastly, and perhaps most crucially, he made whatever he borrowed both new and his own.

One question to consider when using familiar plots is what happens to suspense when you're telling a story of which the outcome is widely known. Shakespeare's audience knew that Prince Hal was going to come to his senses and lead England to victory, and we feel fairly confident that Antonio will not be allowed to die under Shylock's knife. I would suggest that suspense comes in two species, each equally nail-biting. One occurs when we're desperate to know what will happen next as, for me, in Shirley Hazzard's *The Transit of Venus*, or Walter Mosley's *Devil in a Blue Dress*, or Patrick Marber's play *Closer*. The other species, just as potent, is generated when we know roughly what's going to happen but are desperately interested in knowing exactly how it will be brought about. I just reread Thomas Hardy's novel *Tess of the d'Urbervilles*. Even without Hardy's defiant subtitle, *A Pure Woman*, the opening scenes make it clear that Tess is heading toward tragedy, but that didn't stop me from being urgently interested in how it would come about and desperate to avert it.

It's worth noting too that often the outcome is signaled as much by the form as by the content. In *A Midsummer Night's Dream*, even though the play opens with Hermia's father threatening to kill her if she doesn't marry Demetrius, we know we are watching a comedy, a world where bad behavior will not be fatal and love will triumph. A number of years ago I wrote a novel called *Criminals* about a banker who finds a baby at a bus station. The first version ended with the death of the baby, but various readers pointed out that it was too jarring to have a basically comedic novel end so tragically. In revision I revived the baby.

A more straightforward lesson to be learned from Shakespeare's plots is the virtue of having subplots; we often need to tell one story to tell another. *King Lear* would be a shadow of its present self if the actions of Lear and his daughters were not contrasted with the behavior of Gloucester and his sons. In the case of *The Merchant of Venice* the two plots—Shylock's hatred of Antonio and Bassanio's pursuit of Portia—seem to exist in almost equal relation to each other, one advancing the other until they converge. A third plot, the elopement of Shylock's only daughter, Jessica, with Bassanio's friend, Lorenzo, intertwines with the other two. Over and over, the plays demonstrate that a successful subplot is one that is interesting and compelling in its own right, resonates with the main plot appropriately, and intersects with it at the perfect moment. A good subplot also has the virtue of passing time in a way that permits major changes, both internal and external, to occur in the main plot. The scene between Lorenzo and Jessica, from which I quoted earlier, allows enough time to pass for Portia and her maid Nerissa to return from the courtroom to Belmont.

This gift for plotting goes hand in hand with another of Shakespeare's great strengths: his talent for what I call "social characterization." Such were the economics of theater in his time that limiting his cast never seems to have occurred to him. Not for him the monologue, the two-hander, or even the four-hander. Most of his plays have casts of over twenty, and many of them have at least eight substantial roles. This is a large number of characters to bring to life, distinguish, and keep in motion, and of course in performance designers and actors play a key role: Lorenzo is the one in a blue tunic; Regan has spiky hair. But Shakespeare also succeeds in showing each character in his or her social niche. Even his outsiders—Shylock, Edmund—are defined in relation to society. Too often fiction writers, I fear, inadvertently end up making characters quite unrealistically friendless and isolated. But as Portia says, "Nothing is good, I see, without respect." Any painter will tell you that red looks quite different on a blue background than on a violet one.

Another aspect of Shakespeare's skill is the way he introduces his characters so we know at once whether we need to focus on them as individuals or as a group. When, in the second scene of *A Midsummer Night's Dream*, we meet the six rusticals—Peter Quince, Nick Bottom, Francis Flute, Tom Snout, Snug, and Robin Starveling—we know from the way they're introduced that Bottom is the one we should pay attention to, as he exuberantly offers to perform every part in the workmen's play. Meanwhile, Quince, Snout, Flute, Snug, and Starveling are introduced as a group, with Quince in charge. We are invited to appreciate the music of their names and the idiosyncrasies of their characters without worrying about their psyches.

Compare this with the introduction of *Lear's* Edmund, who is also introduced in act 1, scene 2. He has the stage to himself and harangues us in a lengthy soliloquy:

Thou, Nature, art my goddess; to thy law
My services are bound. Wherefore should I
Stand in the plague of custom, and permit
The curiosity of nations to deprive me,
For that I am some twelve or fourteen moonshines
Lag of a brother? Why bastard? wherefore base?

The speech culminates in his ringing declaration: "Now, gods, stand up for bastards!" We never doubt that Edmund is going to play a major part in both the plot and the theme of the play, and we also know at once his position in society. Edmund's character is further deepened by his relationships on the one hand with the vicious sisters, Goneril and Regan, in contrast to whom he seems almost kindly, and on the other with his brother, the virtuous Edgar. Edmund and Edgar are foils to each other; the presence of each throws the other into relief.

While I am invoking the virtues of this kind of characterization, I should also add that our literary heritage offers an abundance of good-sibling-versus-bad-sibling stories—e.g., James Baldwin's wonderful "Sonny's Blues"—or bad, drunken father versus saintly mother—e.g., almost all of Eugene O'Neill's work —so while these are powerful methods of characterization, ones that the reader is quick to recognize and contribute to, we also need to be wary of stereotypes.

I fear I can no longer avoid the most obvious and the most

impossible lesson we can learn from Shakespeare: namely, what can be accomplished by the magnificent, melodious, rigorous, energetic, boisterous, vivid, inventive use of language. Over and over at crucial moments, and also just in passing, the words leap off the page. Titania's forty-line speech, which I quoted from earlier, could be summarized in a single sentence—the natural world is thrown into disarray by her and Oberon's quarrel—but who would wish it a line shorter when the imagery is so playful and deeply pleasurable? In *Henry IV, Part 1*, Hotspur and his allies, the rebels, are poised to fight the king, but there is still time to turn back. Sir Richard Vernon arrives with the news that one of the king's allies, the Earl of Westmoreland, is approaching with seven thousand men. "No harm," says Hotspur. And the king is coming in person, Vernon adds. "He shall be welcome too," says Hotspur. Then Hotspur asks for news of the nimble-footed, madcap Prince of Wales and his comrades, and Vernon, who has previously shown not the least impulse toward poetry, answers:

All furnish'd, all in arms;
All plumed like estridges that with the wind
Bated like eagles having lately bathed;
Glittering in golden coats, like images;
As full of spirit as the month of May,
And gorgeous as the sun at midsummer;
Wanton as youthful goats, wild as young bulls.
I saw young Harry, with his beaver on,
His cuisses on his thighs, gallantly arm'd,
Rise from the ground like feather'd Mercury,

And vaulted with such ease into his seat,
As if an angel dropp'd down from the clouds
To turn and wind a fiery Pegasus
And witch the world with noble horsemanship.

"No more, no more," cries Hostpur.

Everyone in the theater, in the audience and on the stage, knows at that moment that Hotspur's enterprise is doomed. He and Harry are matter and antimatter; they cannot both exist. They must meet, and one of them must die. And it is the music of the language, the gorgeous hyperbole, the cadences that signal this just as much as the content. Once again we are returned to the kind of suspense I mentioned earlier: We know what is going to happen and are filled with dread and anticipation as we watch the battle that follows.

Many young writers, I think, are drawn to what is unkindly called "purple prose," and most find themselves pilloried for their efforts. This kind of lavish, ambitious writing is easy to fail at and easy to make fun of. Almost all my own early work was met with rejections, dozens and dozens of them, that began with the chilling phrase "The prose is beautiful, but . . ." The typical response to this barrage of criticism seems, sadly, not to continue trying to write better, richly metaphorical, muscular prose, but to retreat into something flatter and less adorned. For fiction writers there's no way round having to write some fairly serviceable sentences— "Nina had spent the night in the living-room" (Alice Munro), or "The house wasn't clean" (William Trevor)—but that isn't a reason to give up on the excitement and the possibilities of language.

The notion of a painter who isn't interested in paint is baffling, but many writers (I exclude poets) don't actually seem that interested in language. They are convinced that the interest of their work lies in characterization, plot, and theme. But the plays I'm discussing have survived, in large measure, due to the language Shakespeare invented and put in the mouths of his characters.

I realize he sets a daunting standard and that perhaps I've made it more so by only quoting verse. For those of us who don't naturally fall into iambic pentameter this seems to give him an unfair advantage. Let me add that he also uses prose to admirable, and sometimes surprisingly modern, effect. Here is Sir John Falstaff musing on the field of battle:

> Well, 'tis no matter; honour pricks me on. Yea, but how if honour prick me off when I come on? how then? Can honour set a leg? no: or an arm? no: or take away the grief of a wound? no. Honour hath no skill in surgery, then? no. What is honour? a word. What is in that word honor? air. A trim reckoning! Who hath it? he that died o' Wednesday. Doth he feel it? no. Doth he hear it? no. 'Tis insensible, then? Yea, to the dead. But will it not live with the living? no. Why? detraction will not suffer it. Therefore I'll none of it. Honour is a mere scutcheon: and so ends my catechism.

I don't for a moment mean that we should all be aspiring to write Shakespearian prose. Shakespeare himself, I like to think, would have appreciated the taut, contemporary rhythms of David Mamet and Raymond Carver, the lyricism of Marilynne Robinson and Tony Kushner, the streetwise, braided vernacular of Junot Díaz and Sandra Cisneros. But I do mean to urge that whatever your voice as a writer you should pay more attention to that voice and to amplifying and enriching it by bringing in new words and new metaphors to your vocabulary and to those of your characters.

In conclusion I want to summarize this extremely partial list of what we can learn from Shakespeare: sixteen lessons.

1. Don't be dismayed or surprised if some pieces of work turn out to be rehearsals.
2. Be careful how you repeat yourself, and why.
3. Begin dramatically.
4. Don't keep back the good stuff.
5. Consider beginning in the present.
6. Negotiate your own standards of plausibility.
7. Once you've invented your rules, keep them.
8. Remember the power of appropriate omission. We don't need to take every journey with the characters, make every cup of coffee.
9. Don't overexplain.
10. Be sure that borrowing a plot, character, or situation doesn't seem like theft.
11. Know which kind of suspense your narrative depends on, and use accordingly.
12. Be aware that form and tone govern content.
13. Ask if your plot needs a subplot, or two.
14. Develop your characters both as individuals and in relation to each other. Let the reader know which characters are major and which minor.

15. Be ambitious with your language.

16. Whatever you do, keep making rhymes, lines, puns, clauses, phrases, metaphors, sentences, paragraphs, sonnets, scenes, stories, plays, poems, novels . . .

Shakespeare may not believe in explanations, but he is good at apologies. I'd like to end with one of his most famous, which I also learned when I was nine, lying on the floor of that yellow-paneled drawing room:

> If we shadows have offended,
> Think but this, and all is mended,
> That you have but slumber'd here,
> While these visions did appear.
> And this weak and idle theme,
> No more yielding but a dream,
> Gentles, do not reprehend:
> If you pardon, we will mend.
> And, as I am an honest Puck,
> If we have unearned luck,
> Now to 'scape the serpent's tongue,
> We will make amends ere long:
> Else the Puck a liar call;
> So, good night unto you all.
> Give me your hands, if we be friends,
> And Robin shall restore amends.

LOST IN THE WOODS

ANTONYA NELSON

ONCE UPON A TIME I was listening to NPR's *This American Life*, driving, as I often am, by myself across west Texas. I was lucky to have found any station on the radio, let alone one broadcasting a program with wit and intelligence.

That day's show featured child educator Vivian Paley, who works with preschoolers. In the background, and quoted often, were the children. Their voices, their play, their ideas of narrative were the story's focus. It's Paley's assertion that nearly all education and socialization among children begins with the telling and enacting of stories. They create roles for themselves and others, incorporating their home life, their fantasies, and their friends, and frequently, like a successful improv troupe, they take up any feasible suggestion from a compatriot in order to improve the story.

Paley made a particularly striking comment during the program. She claimed (in a somewhat surprised tone) that children never tire of a very simple story premise. They tolerate this one trajectory, this single narrative arc, time and time and time again: A person (or animal or toy) goes into the woods alone. There, he (she, it) discovers a friend (bear, clown, jack-in-the-box, unicorn, prince) and then is no longer alone. The children announce this premise, follow it through in its predictable plot line, and the listeners sigh happily at its comforting, familiar conclusion.

In a writing workshop, this would likely be viewed as an unfulfilled promise. "What's the conflict?" someone might query. Or, more likely, "What's at stake for this character? What does the character *want*?"

In fact, the character wants companionship and the stakes are actually very high. For if he (she, it) fails to find companionship, then the dark solitude descends. "Hell is other people," claims Sartre. But true hell, maybe, is having the certain knowledge of your isolation dramatized for you. We die alone; but until then, we need friends.

Moreover, we need that special friend. There's Mother, first, and then, perhaps, Dog. Nana. Siblings suffice, for a while, and then Best Friends. Teammates. Roommates. Lovers. Spouses, for many, maybe most. And then children, sons and daughters and grandchildren. Those are the conventional human entanglements, and they often succeed at fulfilling the requirement for intimacy, companionship, understanding, love.

But sometimes they don't. And if they don't, then a person might find herself in a dark woods. Alone. Dante's *Inferno* begins with that premise. Here is the beginning of Canto One: "Midway in our life's journey, I went astray from the straight road and woke to find myself alone in a dark wood. How shall I

say what wood that was! I never saw so drear, so rank, so arduous a wilderness! Its very memory gives a shape to fear."

This narrator is in need of someone, or something. His lostness,
in this instance, is so profound as to intimate suicide. He wants
rescue. He requires that missing person, or animal, or presence.

Someone lost in the woods might decide that a magic lantern
will answer his prayer; he might turn to a shapely bottle and
investigate its contents. Dante needed Virgil. Alice goes down
a hole in the ground, chasing a rabbit and ingesting treats, to
discover what she needs. Dorothy Gale, bereft of her companion
Toto, takes a lump to the head, and thus begins her journey, her
quest for understanding and assistance. Both Alice's and Dorothy's adventures are about the search for companionship and the
return to home. Shenanigans and peril, in each instance, ensue.
Lessons are learned. A reason for continuing presents itself. And
in the end, as in the end of the children's much simpler tales,
the character emerges from the woods (hell, underground, Oz,
desertion) intact and less alone.

For ten years Odysseus was headed home to his wife; like him,
Penelope longed for their reunion. In Sofia Coppola's film *Lost
in Translation*, Bill Murray is lonely in Japan. Lucky for him,
there's Scarlett Johansson, also lonely. Tokyo is a dark woods,
and they are lucky and relieved to have found each other. In *A
Passage to India*, Indian Dr. Aziz stumbles into the mosque and
discovers British Mrs. Moore there. At first he is angry—a white
woman in his temple!—but E. M. Forster gently marries these
characters, who are in no way romantic mates. They are spiritual
mates. They have linked sensibilities; their hooking up is a holier

union than most. *A Passage to India* is predicated on the impossible, yet achingly instinctive desire to "only connect."

One member of Paley's preschool class is "The Boy Who Would Be a Helicopter." He is probably vaguely autistic, high-functioning, yet solitary to a degree considered irregular. His playmates invite him into their games (which are ongoing, morphing narratives), but he stubbornly resists. He loves his helicopter. He would like to be a helicopter himself so that he could fly with his friend, the machine, and have adventures. Machine adventures. Rescue missions, yet with rotors, so that, perhaps, there wouldn't be hugging involved.

While he will not join the other children in their communal storytelling, the overarching theme of Paley's book, titled *The Boy Who Would Be a Helicopter*, is his eventual inclusion in their games. That is, he is a figure lost in a kind of woods, alone although surrounded by peers, and the year of his life Paley portrays is, mostly, about his finally permitting himself—by the persistent and charitable and heroic gestures of his classmates—to be included, to be found. This conclusion is a happy one because he has, in some way, been rescued from the dark woods of his probable autism. He has been subtly and gently socialized, brought a few steps outside the limited solitude of his affliction and inside the hearty heat of his preschool mates. And although he wouldn't have been able to name a desire for this, it is clear to the reader, through Paley's descriptions, that the boy *did* want to connect with the other children. He simply had no idea how to go about doing so.

Many successful and satisfying adult narratives follow this basic pattern: a marriage plot in which the participants are first challenged by the problem of locating each other and then that of figuring out that they're meant to be together, never mind all of the hubbub surrounding their inevitable fated coupledom. Misunderstandings, lasting many tense chapters, fuel the suspense; the majority of the text may indulge in a kind of mild chaos, yet the conclusion is that of a new order, an end to chaos and upheaval, engendered by the author to the great relief and satisfaction of the characters as well as that of the readers.

For many readers, a happy ending is a requirement. I don't mean a simplistic happy ending, but one that's been earned—by hardship and mishap, by dedicated labor and determination and faith, by good character overcoming bad luck. My own tolerance for happy endings, however, is very low. I don't believe in them. I think this may explain why I approve of short stories, in general, more often than I do of novels. Novels tend toward the restored and ordered world; they tend toward happiness, hard-earned and bittersweet as it may be, while short stories tend otherwise. They are less conclusive, less closed, less ordered and unchaotic.

The story I want to use to tie together these, so far, rather diffuse and disconnected thoughts is William Trevor's "Folie à Deux." Essentially, the story is as follows: Wilby, in Paris for an annual stamp-collecting vacation, eats at a restaurant where he observes a minion employee of the restaurant who seems familiar to him. Through back story, the reader learns that when Wilby was a child, he had a friend he visited on the Irish coast in the summertime. He believes the stranger he recognizes in the French café is this long-ago friend, Anthony.

At age nine, Wilby and Anthony shared a strange episode. Anthony's father was always interested in what makes the world tick, and he encouraged in the boys a love of knowledge, of inquiry. In this spirit, they had adventured along their coastal paradise, discovering a secret cove and finding a yellow raft that they allowed Anthony's old dog to sleep on. One day they put the ancient dog onto the raft and set it in the sea. Away the dog goes, gamely floating, then barking, then wailing, as the boys scrabble over the rocks up to the top of a cliff, watching the dog sail away. A few days later the dog's body washes up on shore.

The boys do not discuss this event. Anthony becomes reclusive, solitary, distant, and strange. As teenagers, the boys attend school together, but Anthony is no longer close to Wilby. Not to him, nor to his parents, nor to any other person. And then he simply disappears.

This disappearance is eventually understood by family and friends to be a death. Like the dog on the raft, Anthony has floated away from the social shore, although no body is ever washed resolutely back. Time passes. Wilby is now a middle-aged man who inherited his family's wine business, which he has sold. The proceeds allow him to pursue his stamp collecting, and this brings him to Paris and to the current awkward reunion between him and Anthony, accidental and unacknowledged as it is. Anthony is not dead. Upon leaving the café, Wilby is troubled by the possibility of Anthony's being a kitchen worker and he creates a fantasy to explain Anthony's choice. Anthony is an exemplary worker; he does the job of two. He seldom speaks; he frequently neglects to pick up his paycheck. In the sleepless imagination Wilby experiences that night, he transforms Anthony's perfectionist labors in the kitchen into acts of penance. Anthony has not ever been able to forgive or excuse the act he committed, the act that Wilby also participated in, however innocently and guilelessly they engaged in the experiment. It was not meant unkindly; yet the fact of an animal's death, as a result, still inflicts guilt on Anthony. Wilby does not suffer this guilt. The difference in the boys' responses (never discussed, never articulated) is Wilby's explanation for the estrangement that ensued between them. It is also the explanation for Anthony's estrangement from everything once familiar, his denial of a "normal" future life.

This reminder of the severed friendship, the rupture of intimacy, disturbs Wilby because it forces him to acknowledge something in himself that he does not admire; an act that Wilby has chosen to excuse, explain, expiate, and forget, that he has overcome, is one that Anthony has refused to excuse, explain, expiate, or forgive in himself—or so Wilby conjectures—which suggests that Wilby has moved ahead in his life by positing an exculpatory story. Through the process of his conjecture concerning his old friend, Wilby must confront an element of his own character. He must confess that he likes himself less than he does his old friend. Despite the ostracism, the solitude and suffering of Anthony, Wilby sees something discomfitingly shameful in his own capacity to forgive himself. He has not judged himself harshly enough, and the only one in the world he can imagine understanding this is Anthony. And even that understanding is of something so subtle and transient, so ephemeral and intangible, so distant, that the reader is left pleasantly puzzled, unsure whether to dictate guilt upon Wilby or not.

The story takes its title from a rare psychiatric syndrome in which a symptom of psychosis (particularly a paranoid or delusional belief) is transmitted from one individual to another (*folie à deux* means "a madness shared by two"). This shared psychosis seems, to me, an inversion of the "friend in the woods" narrative I presented earlier. That is, the sensibility located and adored, in this instance, is not a helpful union but a frightening one. To share a psychosis is not the ideal sharing of a sensibility. The friend you find in the woods is not supposed to make the woods a more frightening place.

When Bill Murray and Scarlett Johansson meet in *Lost in Translation*, the viewer has the gratification of witnessing their growing friendship. The story is shaped, more or less, by their meeting, their blooming intimacy, and their eventual separation. This design, a frame that the director provides for the movie, is satisfying and knowable by the viewer. Still, inside this story lurks a lingering mystery embodied in the small gesture, at the film's close, when Bill Murray whispers in Scarlett Johansson's ear. What does he say? We don't know. Whatever is between them is locked resolutely and utterly inside the mystery of their intimacy.

The question posed at the beginning of *A Passage to India* is can an Englishman be a true friend to an Indian? The book's overall trajectory is the opposite one of the marriage plot. In the Marabar Caves, at the heart of the story, each individual encounters the cave's echo. For each, it is interpreted differently. For the reader, no clear explanation is ever provided by the omniscient narrator. Like Coppola, Forster honors the notion of unknowableness, of genuine and necessary mystery. The caves represent an episode of inverted intimacy, a place where the characters do not connect (as they did earlier, in the mosque). The rupture that occurs there is the book's inverse trajectory; the characters lost in the woods, although together, do not find each other. The book closes with the same outcome: Dr. Aziz and Cyril Fielding, although they wish to be friends, cannot overcome the greater odds against it. There is quite evidently the desire to locate the friend in the woods, but the desire is thwarted by various issues. The very earth and sky conspire against a friendship predicated on the unequal power relations of empire. "Only connecting" is much harder than it looks, and Forster's emphasis on the ache that concludes the book is somehow more poignant and satisfying and true, to this reader, than the opposite outcome would have been. True friendship, Forster seems to argue, depends on equality, as well as some ineffable other element, something nearly magical.

Forster wrote his novel as a reaction to, and perhaps an interrogation into, the ecstatic poem Walt Whitman conceived when the Suez Canal first opened:

> *Passage to India!*
> *Lo, soul, seest thou not God's purpose from the first?*
> *The earth to be spann'd, connected by network,*
> *The races, neighbors, to marry and be given in marriage,*
> *The oceans to be cross'd, the distant brought near,*
> *The lands to be welded together.*

Whitman was making a wish, based in the desire for borderlessness, for being united rather than divided, for the "woods" of the world to be happily coinhabited by its multicultural members. Forster feels otherwise and sets out a sort of empirical study of human nature to demonstrate the impossibility of union. What's "lost" in the instance of *A Passage to India* is the connection that each party seeks. What's "lost" in Trevor's story is a connection that once existed. By the end of "Folie à Deux," Wilby feels not only the loss of his friend Anthony but also the loss (or, perhaps, the nonexistence) of his own moral center. He has excused their shared past action, but he believes that Anthony has been incapable of doing so. The moral absence that Wilby experiences in himself is the true source of his lostness. It's nothing less than a spiritual vacuum, albeit a very small one and one that the reader is prepared to defend against, to step into and redeem, to assure Wilby that he need not feel bad, he need not judge himself so harshly. The power of this story is its ability to make the reader complicit with Wilby: what the boys did was not meant unkindly. They were not "evil" in the conventional definition of the word. In a world (and ours is precisely this world) that is prepared to forgive and understand any and all behavior, where does one locate moral certainty? Wilby locates it in Anthony and finds himself lacking. That the reader is more likely to be a Wilby than an Anthony is why the story resonates so profoundly.

It occurs to me that many of the most mysterious and enduring stories told are ones wherein a moral quandary is presented in the form of deciding whether or not to betray a friendship. Such a trajectory begins with the location of the friend in the woods, but does not end there. This is a narrative that moves beyond the marriage plot to the subsequent divorce, or that requires its protagonist to make the excruciating choice between remaining loyal to the friend and doing the socially understood "right" thing. Either action has its cost, and the reader is left uneasily lodged between that proverbial rock and hard place. Which is to say, lonely. That the reader of such stories is included in a conspiracy of intimacy—that she roots, eventually, either for an outcome other than the inevitable or for the risky, wrong move—is to put her in the "wrong." I think this is precisely the position in which Wilby finds himself, at story's end, in "Folie a Deux."

Fortunately, since the reader has been through the woods with him, he isn't, finally, alone.

PERFORMING SURGERY WITHOUT ANESTHESIA

CHRIS OFFUTT

AWHILE BACK, I was teaching a class in which the average age was, I believe, twenty-three. And so I thought I'd go back through my files—because I compulsively save everything—and look at the stories I'd written when I was twenty-three. I chose the best one out of a lousy bunch. There were three characters, two guys and a woman—a love triangle. One of the guys was a drug smuggler; I thought that was pretty cool. The setting was a bar, which I also thought was very cool. But as I re-read the story, I was astounded. Nothing happened. The characters sat in a bar. The action consisted only of drinking, smoking, leaning, and looking; the rest of the time they talked.

I realize now that what I was doing then was refusing to revise. I didn't know how. I was afraid of it. I was polishing; I wasn't revising. The result was a highly polished second draft that was just as junky as the original. To be a successful writer you have to develop two skills that are polar opposites: generating a first draft and revising. The first draft requires an unbelievable subjectivity;

you pour all your emotions into it, you stake your life on every word, you make yourself completely vulnerable on the page. You write in that white-hot heat like a drug experience. Every time I start something new I'm terrified that it's going to be no good, that I can't write anymore, that I've lost it. I experience extreme self-consciousness. But if I commit to the process and engage in it, at some point the self-consciousness and the terror dissipate and the story kicks in. What I try to do in a first draft is to follow every impulse. I throw everything but the kitchen sink into the narrative, then I throw in the kitchen sink, fill it with dishes, turn on the water, and let it overflow. By then, I have become enthused by it, I stay up late, I don't go to the bathroom, I don't eat, I drink more coffee (maybe then I go the bathroom, I guess). Then I become aware that I am approaching the ending, and that's another situation that is fraught with anxiety because I don't want it to end. I've been living with these people for a while—I know them and feel close to them. They're like guests I hope will stay longer. Plus, finishing means I will have to start all over again with the terror of something new. So I continue until at some point I realize I've got to write an end scene. And I think, "I've got to write an end line, a killer end line, a glittering, lyrical, beautiful, charming end line that reverberates all the way back through the story." And I do, and that end line has nothing to do with the story, but it sure does look good. It's like a beautiful gigantic neon sign that says: ENDING!

By the end I believe that I've written something absolutely brilliant—probably the best thing I've ever written, maybe better than anything anyone's ever written. I love that feeling; it lasts until the next morning, when I look at the work again and realize it's a piece of crap. I feel bad for that, but I feel even worse for having thought it was so brilliant. For me, that's pretty much the process of generating a first draft. I think it's important to feel that way, even though I now know it's a false genius. Still, I get to feel that "geniusness" briefly. Overnight. A sleeping genius.

The process of revision is drastically different. It is draining the sink and seeing what's in there, which is usually a mess. Revising requires a cruel and ruthless objectivity with which you essentially perform surgery on *yourself* without anesthesia. In order to have something successful to revise, you must make yourself vulnerable on the page, particularly in the first draft. The more you make yourself vulnerable—you make yourself personably vulnerable on the page—the more you're going to care about what you're doing (and if you don't care about it, you may as well hang it up) and the more you're going to reach the reader. If you make yourself vulnerable, that vulnerability will translate into empathy—reader empathy. So if you've done the first part of the job correctly, you are emotionally engaged at a deep level with the first draft and there is no way you can go back into it and revise successfully because you care too much about it, you're too engaged. So then, how do you develop the skill of cruel and ruthless objectivity?

One of the ways that I do it is to go away from the work, leave it alone. If you get some distance and time from the first draft, you can look at it objectively. It's the same with a broken heart. Think about it: a little distance and time will heal your broken heart; a little distance and time will allow you to look at a draft and figure out what it is you're doing. After finishing the first draft I'll look through it and fix the surface errors. I make it semi-legible and correct the punctuation, spelling, and grammar. I often change the names. Then I print it out and put it away for a while.

After that, the only way for me to disengage emotionally in order to obtain the necessary objectivity is to write something new. I'm always working on multiple projects—this serves the overall work. It's not because I can't finish anything or I'm unfocused. When I start another story and become emotionally engaged with that one, then I can return to earlier ones and look at them on their own terms.

I think the word *revision* means *to see again* or *to look again*. Most people don't do that; as I've said, they polish. You must learn to re-see your work. And that often means noticing what the story is really about, what it's become. Not what you thought it was, or what you wanted it to be.

Here's a mistake a lot of writers make: You say to yourself, "I'm trying to write a father-son story, and so I'm going to keep focusing on that because that was my plan." It doesn't matter what you were trying to write. You have to be able to look at the first draft and see what it has developed into on its own. Maybe the father winds up being more interesting and the story is focused on him, but you've written it from the son's point of view. Well, you have to recognize that and say, "Ok. Time to shift the focus. Time to make it about the father rather than the son."

Try to see what the story is, rather than what you are trying to force it into. If you've done that first draft successfully, you've tapped into your intuition, your impulses, your unconscious, your problems of the day, whatever emotional state you're in. It's there; it has translated into prose on the page. Now you need to forget what it is you've tried to do, look at the story, see what it has become, and begin to attempt to fix it, to revise it, to improve it. I was always afraid to revise, because I was afraid I would make a story worse. But I've learned that it's possible to improve a story and that I can't make it worse, because I can always go back to the way it was.

I've developed a system for the revision process that may or may not work for you, but it's systematic and makes the task a little easier. Once I finish a draft, I print it out. I don't mess with it. I number and date it. I revise it with pen on that copy. I put those changes into the electronic file. Then I put the hard copy into a folder in a drawer. I print the version with the changes and label it: draft two, with a date. I revise that draft in pen and put the changes into the electronic file. I continue this process over time, months and years.

As a result I always have the current draft on the computer and all prior drafts at my disposal arranged chronologically. Many times, at draft ten or twelve I'm completely lost; I have no idea what's going on. I've cut it, I've changed it, I've chopped it, I've shortened it, I've opened it up. I've lost track of what's going on. So I go back to that first draft, the one in the drawer, to see what is happening. Very often I will bring a lot of the earlier ideas back into the story. Having multiple drafts on the computer is not as successful as you'd think. First of all, you've got to remember which draft is which. Secondly, you can't open up more than one or two on the screen and have any luck keeping track of them. At least, I can't. That doesn't work for me.

In the early stage of revision, you need to look at structure, point of view, plot, flashback, and exposition. These are just a few elements—there are probably more—but these are the big ones that you must examine and make sure, before you go forward, that they're serving the story, not the writer. Many, many stories collapse because the writer is trying to make it easier on himself. Don't do that. Serve the story. Writers are smart people facing a tough job. Writers are smart enough to figure out shortcuts, but you must avoid this impulse. There are no shortcuts in art.

Once you get the early decisions squared away, trim the opening. One of the first things I do is cut the first few pages because in those pages I'm preparing to write, I'm priming the pump of narrative, I'm doing calisthenics. It's crucial to figure out where a story takes off. I'm sure you've heard people say, "Ah, the story really takes off for me on page four." Well, there's your opening. There's nothing worse than having a thirty-five-page story and people say, "Really, I love it. It begins on page thirty-two." I've done that, and they were right. Those first thirty-two pages were me warming up. Beginnings get bogged down, which is natural because in the process of writing and revising you always start at the beginning and work through to the end, so the beginning receives more attention. I also often cut the last half page to two pages because they have nothing to do with the story. The actual narrative—the story proper—has already happened. I have cut thousands of pages from my work, but those cut pages were necessary to the final draft. To me, the final product is like an iceberg: you only see ten percent of the actual work, but that other ninety percent is still there.

Each time you approach a story and read it to yourself to try and revise it, you know what's supposed to happen, you anticipate what's going to happen within your own story. When you start doing that it becomes difficult to look at the work objectively: "Oh I'm coming up on the action scene—okay—I'm going to start reading faster, it doesn't matter, I love the action part, I'm not going to bear down on the language or the sentences quite as hard." Look at your sentences very carefully—look at the consistency of tone, style, and language and vary your sentence structure. Do whatever it takes to keep the sentences hopping and to avoid monotony.

On a structural level, change the order of scenes. Move things around. Switch the opening and closing and see what happens. Do you have a linear structure or a circular structure? Why do you have that one, and does it serve the story? Does it serve the situation? If there's not a lot of action or much of the story is set inside the main character's head, then circular may be more effective. But if it's a story about a guy who has a fight with his boss, steals a car, and robs a 7–Eleven, then linear might be better. Combine characters—that's another trick I do constantly. If you have too many, the narrative becomes ungainly. When I have too many characters, I combine two into one and suddenly the new character has more dimension. Avoid too much exposition: stories get bogged down by exposition. Writers are writers, which means we're constantly writing notes to ourselves as we write: we write about what we're going to write, we write about what's going to happen, we write comments about the characters, etc. But you don't need all that information in the final draft. These are notes to the self that are valuable to the writing process, but they interfere with the narrative. I worked on a father-son story in which I started with the grandparents and the great grandfather. Finally, after years, I realized I only needed to write about the father and the son; I didn't need their family lineage in there. It was important for me personally to understand them, but not for making a piece of art. I'm not saying these are rules; I just think that to get going in this difficult activity, you can simplify some things. You can make it easier on yourself, especially in the early stages. I don't mean shortcuts! I mean lessen the burden you bear during the process.

After six months or five years, you might have something worthwhile and you can start polishing, by which I mean making sure you've got the right verb, cutting out words that repeat, making sure you don't have two similes in the same short paragraph. If you've used adverbs, look at them carefully. Adverbs are the weakest words; verbs are the strongest. Many, many times I've found that I have the wrong verb so I'm attempting to cheat and modify the wrong verb by using an adverb.

I rely on the first draft to see what it is I'm writing about. The first draft is a difficult step in order to have something to play with. Then I look at it objectively, see what the story has become, and revise it. As a result of committing to writing and trying to operate from this standpoint, I'm not afraid of revision anymore. In fact I prefer it. I have one story with drafts that run back eighteen years—but it's getting better.

And one final tip: just write. There are no rules. Experiment and learn. Don't pay any attention to someone who tells you what you should be doing.

(MIS)ADVENTURES IN POETRY

D. A. POWELL

So MUCH OF the time, new poets are looking for the proper turn of phrase, the way to translate their ideas into poems—they reach after metaphors that will approximate a sense of the world as close as possible to their own experience. But often it's the inexact, the awful, the mistaken linguistic turn that manages to say the right thing because it unmoors us from our perceived relationship to the subject about which we're trying to write. Often, poetry is enriched by saying precisely what we didn't set out to say.

What is the hidden light of discovery within the poem? Have we given the reader a new experience of the world through language? In a letter to Robert Creeley, William Carlos Williams wrote that "bad art is . . . that which does not serve in the continual service of cleansing the language upon all fixations upon dead, stinking dead, usages of the past. Sanitation and hygiene or sanitation that we may have hygienic writing." The poet's job is to clean up words so that they appear fresh and new in the context of the poem. Etel Adnan said once in conversation that she felt that words are like coins—they grow dirty and lackluster with repeated handling. But poets give language a good scrub; they polish up the coins so that we are struck by their beauty. In his poem "Spring and All," Williams writes:

By the road to the contagious hospital
under the surge of the blue
mottled clouds driven from the
northeast—a cold wind. Beyond, the
waste of broad, muddy fields
brown with dried weeds, standing and fallen

patches of standing water
the scattering of tall trees

All along the road the reddish
purplish, forked, upstanding, twiggy
stuff of bushes and small trees
with dead, brown leaves under them
leafless vines—

Lifeless in appearance, sluggish
dazed spring approaches—

They enter the new world naked,
cold, uncertain of all
save that they enter. All about them
the cold, familiar wind—

Now the grass, tomorrow
the stiff curl of wildcarrot leaf
One by one objects are defined—
It quickens: clarity, outline of leaf

But now the stark dignity of
entrance—Still, the profound change
has come upon them: rooted, they
grip down and begin to awaken

None of this language is unfamiliar; these are words we know.
But the combinations surprise us. "The contagious hospital" is
not how we're used to hearing that particular modifier and that
particular noun grouped together, yet we certainly understand
the relationship between them. Nor are we used to hearing the
underbrush and weeds described as "the reddish / purplish, forked,
upstanding, twiggy / stuff of bushes and small trees," but there
is something lush and overgrown about the way these modifiers
bump against one another. Even the idea of "cold, familiar wind"
seems *unfamiliar*, though once we hear the phrase, we understand
its certainty. As "one by one objects are defined," we imagine them
with a clarity that is made possible by the language, even though it
might be the first time we've heard the words brought together.

Of course, clarity is not necessarily the goal of a poem; in
fact, a poem more often contains a strong element of mystery so
that we are called back to the words and asked to ruminate upon
them, deepening our sense of how it is that they discover their
meanings. Even a phrase made up of the most ordinary words

can, in the hands of a gifted poet, draw us into our souls to find the path that the poem has led us to. Robert Duncan writes of his metaphorical meadow as "a place of first permission, / everlasting omen of what is." These are not unfamiliar words whose definitions are hiding in antique volumes of obscure dictionaries, nor are they cryptic slang or jargon that must be cracked like code in order to be understood. And yet, I cannot say that there is any better way for me to explain the complexity of "a place of first permission, everlasting omen of what is" except to repeat the phrase—it is its own best version of itself; ultimately, an idea unparaphraseable. Perhaps this is the pinnacle of poetic imagination: to construct the line in such a way that it is tonic, plenary, irreducible.

Hart Crane's first "Voyages" poem is perhaps the finest example of a diction that exfoliates and deepens upon successive readings. It is made largely of commonplace words that, in methodical combination, create an extraordinary layering:

Above the fresh ruffles of the surf
Bright striped urchins flay each other with sand.
They have contrived a conquest for shell shucks,
And their fingers crumble fragments of baked weed
Gaily digging and scattering.

And in answer to their treble interjections
The sun beats lightning on the waves,
The waves fold thunder on the sand;
And could they hear me I would tell them:

O brilliant kids, frisk with your dog,
Fondle your shells and sticks, bleached
By time and the elements; but there is a line
You must not cross nor ever trust beyond it
Spry cordage of your bodies to caresses
Too lichen-faithful from too wide a breast.
The bottom of the sea is cruel.

Note how the poem proceeds from the surface of the water to the bed of the sea. Each successive line holds a portent of doom: note the violence of "flay," "conquest," "crumble," "scattering," "interjections," "beats lightning," "fold thunder" . . . all of the energy building into the speaker's turn toward warning. Then the soft tones lulling us, as if the waves themselves are singing a lullaby: "brilliant kids," "fondle your shells," "time and the elements," "cross" and "trust," "cordage," "caresses," "faithful," and "a breast." The gentle sounds of the words and the ways in which they gesture toward beauty set up the shiver that comes at the end of the stanza: "The bottom of the sea is cruel."

Elements of the sea populate the poem at each step, from the punning "urchins" to the "shells and sticks, bleached / By time." Even the bodies of the "urchins" are described as "cordage," a word whose definitions include the rigging on a ship and the measure of wood (driftwood?). Note, too, how sound changes in the poem, from the "treble interjections" of the children to the thundering waves and finally to the monodic voice that cannot quite rise to the prophetic level—after all, the children cannot hear the speaker, and so his voice becomes internal, somber, baritone as it works through the flat tones of monosyllabic entreaties ("frisk with your dog," "your shells and sticks, bleached / By time," and "but there is a line / You must not cross") coupled with the trochees that provide the intermittent, dying fall.

Certainly there is skill evident in the design of such an elaborate network of sound and sense; however, I'd imagine that Crane discovered some of the words of the poem by accident. Crane's logophile mind understood the possibilities of randomly attained words—in "The Tunnel," snatches of conversation invade the poem:

> The phonographs of hades in the brain
> Are tunnels that re-wind themselves, and love
> A burnt match skating in a urinal—
> Somewhere above Fourteenth TAKE THE EXPRESS
> To brush some new presentiment of pain—
>
> "But I want service in this office SERVICE
> I said—after
>   the show she cried a little afterwards but—"

These voices are set against the jingles of Madison Avenue, the argot of tearoom sex and the highly lyrical rhymes and sonorous phrases of Victoriana clashing with modernism. Much of the material in Crane's poems is gathered piecemeal, with the sensibility of a magpie that fetches bright, shiny baubles and weaves them into its nest. The texture of the poems is largely determined by what's available in the larger world of the poet.

Sometimes, a typo provides the portal to discovery. For example, we know that one of Crane's most famous lines, the first line of the second "Voyages" poem, came as a mistake. "Voyages II" begins, "—And yet this great wink of eternity." Originally, the line read "great wing of eternity," but upon seeing the typographical mistake, Crane recognized how much more original and problematic wink made the poem. *Wink* is akin to *twinkling*, a faint echo of the eternity contained in 1 Corinthians 15:52: "In a moment, in the twinkling of an eye, at the last trump: for the trumpet shall sound, and the dead shall be raised incorruptible, and we shall be changed." At the same time, the wink is a come-on, a seduction by a possible lover, as if the eternal itself is our paramour. Invoking the eye rather than the bird, this turn of phrase resists the obviousness of *wing*. It challenges our notions of a conventional eternity by avoiding the obvious connection with angels, doves, and other creatures of the air.

Haines Eason wrote a poem with the following lines:

"You telescope for
faint novas. For the tremor that was a billion gasps.
Though, these too retrograde
as the science of how we all
migration into winter."

Except, instead of *though*, he typed the word *tough*, so that the poem reads:

"You telescope for
faint novas. For the tremor that was a billion gasps.
Tough, these too retrograde
as the science of how we all
migration into winter."

When he realized the dropped h, he immediately understood it not as a mistake but as an accident of discovery. Closer to the intent of the tone of the poem, *tough* hardens the mind of the speaker at the place where it needs to harden, where science slips from the human study to the consideration of the larger world, where "we all migration into winter."

Sometimes the mistake is not typographical but an error in translation. Reading one's own handwriting, one might easily misinterpret an original impulse for another somehow better suited to the poem. I call this the "mondegreen effect," after Sylvia Wright's coinage of the term mondegreen to describe the phenomenon of mishearing a song lyric. In her childhood, Wright had heard a tune in which some lines seemed to be "They hae slain the Earl Amurray / and Lady Mondegreen." It wasn't until years later that Wright realized the lyric was "They hae slain the Earl of Moray / and laid him on the green."

We all have mondegreens. In his novel *Bedrooms Have Windows*, Kevin Killian has his main character overhear a child praying, "Surely good Mrs. Murphy will follow me all of my days." And the poet Robert Duncan said that when he was growing up he interpreted the line "Gladly the cross I'd bear," from the hymn "Keep Thou I May," as being about a vision-challenged ursine named Gladly. In his book *Tiny Courts*, poet David Bromige has a woman say that she's reading a book entitled "Civilization and Its Discotheques."

Tristan Tzara said, "We have always made mistakes, but the greatest mistakes are the poems we have written." Perhaps the first and greatest impulse of poetry is to misstep, mistake, mishear. We apprehend the world in a way which is inherently suspect, and only through suspect language can we approximate that view. To mishear or to misread is to misapprehend. Perhaps, in that way, it is to see the world or the word for the first time. Think of Gertrude Stein puzzling over the phrase "Let's make our flour meal and meat in Georgia," wondering if what she's reading is poetry or prose, much less what the phrase means, what it sounds like it means, and what the sounds themselves mean. No wonder, then, that she's able to take the name of the futurist Marinetti and weave it into a poem that asks, "should I marry Netty?" Or to elongate the word *sweetie* into "sweet sweet tea."

Take the familiar from your work and make it unfamiliar. "Revise toward strangeness," Rachel Zucker once advised my students, and I would hasten to add, "Revise toward discovery." After all, if a poem says everything you wanted it to say, it's probably not a poem at all; it's a shopping list, an essay, a diary entry, a first draft. In the aforementioned "Voyages" poem, Crane could easily have written, "The sun shines on the surface of the water," and we would probably never remember that particular phrase. Instead, he writes, "The sun beats lightning on the waves," so that we see that light in its own particulars, separate from all the ways in which light has cast its gaze upon the waters of other shores. Crane achieves a fierceness, a jaggedness for his lighting; he makes us see the effect of light upon waves as if we're seeing it for the very first time.

Tzara writes, "Logic no longer guides us, and though it is convenient to have dealings with, it has become impotent, a deceptive glimmer . . . and we consider it from henceforth a light that has failed forever." I don't know that I go the whole way with that notion, but there is certainly a case to be made in saying that the sentence, the syllogism, the line, the stanza—these are all traps, linguistically, with certain built-in expectations and inevitabilities. A sentence must invariably include time; a line must ultimately come to an end. The trick is to spring the trap.

One might state the case slightly differently, as a case of difficulty or complexity. "Complicate your life as much as you want," says Gertrude Stein, "eventually it will simplify." We live inside a complication, the way a previous generation—long past—might have lived inside a circadian clock. We don't die from the dread diseases of our time; we die from complications—these are forces most dominant in our world, like the fates of yore or the factories of the industrial age: analogous to our traffic, both physical and mental. Let the complication inform the work. It's already suggested by the very act of writing and living in the world: I have complications; that is the situation from which I must speak. To ignore is to deny.

The Oulipo poet Jacques Roubaud says that the poet is a rat who builds his own maze and then must find his way out. I'm afraid too often poets don't build mazes at all; they build corridors with well-marked entrances and exits; they proceed through the doors as quickly as possible and assume they've accomplished something. I say, "Get lost." Build a true maze, a poem that doesn't have a clear path. Be willing to wander in the labyrinth and risk encountering the Minotaur. At least if you fail, the scholar who finds your bones will be able to ask, "Did he starve or was he eaten?"

Young writers often ask me if I worry about sounding this way or that way—too obscure, too direct, too sentimental, too harsh, too comic, too sad, too erudite, too colloquial—when I'm writing. What this question suggests to me is that these writers are thinking about what a poem will be like *before* they've actually sat down to write it. When a poem is gestating in your mind, you can't go in for an ultrasound. How can you know what a poem will be like before it arrives on the page? Worry about tone, yes, worry about language. But take these worries on at the time of revision, not at the time of first vision.

I do not use the idea of gestation haphazardly. There is more than a metaphorical connection between birth and language. We grow into language much the same way that we grow into our bodies. Julien Torma writes, "The first cries are no more than mechanical effects produced by the functioning of the body. Even the first words are still not words. The child discovers autonomous reality only by lying. Then the word is used for itself; it becomes meaning. Game or chance, it matters little: the child says 'bobo,' 'hurt.' Right away (and if it hasn't felt any pain) the whole sequence of cajoleries and sugary consolations is triggered off. It is understandable that, after this discovery, the child tries the experiment again, the better to assure itself of the wonderful efficacy of the Word. And if it loves lying so much (that joy in its eyes), that is because it is savoring the happiness and the power of the cabalistic intelligence: the word is creative."

Poets are liars who get away with it. One of the best things you can do in order to liberate yourself from the empirical realm of language is to lie in the poem. Does anyone think for a moment that H.D. is giving us the gospel in her Helen of Troy poem?

All Greece hates
the still eyes in the white face,
the lustre as of olives
where she stands,
and the white hands.

All Greece reviles
the wan face when she smiles,
hating it deeper still
when it grows wan and white,
remembering past enchantments
and past ills.

Greece sees, unmoved,
God's daughter, born of love,
the beauty of cool feet
and slenderest knees,
could love indeed the maid,
only if she were laid,
white ash amid funereal cypresses.

This poem is built of choices made through imagination. H.D. speaks for a country whose mind she cannot know about a subject beyond her ken. She doesn't say, "I've read books on Ilium and this is what they said." She says, "In my mind's eye, I know this."

"Tell all the truth, but tell it slant." Don't suppose for one moment that a poem has any more authority than the emperor of ice cream or the rabbit who gets to be the king of ghosts. To quote E. E. Cummings, "Every artist's strictly illimitable country is himself." You might as well make the rules and set down the laws as you prefer them; no one else is going to pay them the heed you've envisioned. Unacknowledged legislators. The hierophants of an unapprehended inspiration. Those who utter great and wise things that they themselves do not understand. The sibyls. This is what poets get to be, should they dare to enter that place of first permission.

I'd like to offer a few ways of dislocating the self in relation to the poem. Some are simple, some require a little work.

Dream. And let dreaming be a portal to the unknown.

Forget the poem you've written and then try to write it afresh. Afterward, you can compare the two versions and see what discoveries you made in having to take the same journey twice.

Put the poem across the table from you and eavesdrop upon it, as if it's the poem of someone else whose work you might admire. Don't be afraid to reach over and mark suggestions in the margin.

Fold the poem in half lengthwise. Read only one half and try to make the connections from line to line without relying upon the original.

Systematically replace a troubling word with others that are culled from favorite novels until you hit upon a new way of conceiving the image or idea that had you stuck.

Cut the poem to bits and rearrange it. (See Tristan Tzara's "How to Make a Dadaist Poem.")

Translate your work into English, using paraphrase.

Translate your work into Portuguese, using Babel Fish—then translate it back into English, using the same tool.

Write your poem blindfolded or in the dark, so that you're forced to reinterpret your own handwriting.

Write the poem with your left hand (if right-handed) or right (if left-handed).

Write the poem that undoes everything within the poem—make it into its own Bizarro reflection.

Remember that Wallace Stevens said that all poems are experimental. Live in the experiment. Don't think of a poem as finished; think of it, perhaps, as a lover you've abandoned. There will be times when you'll come back and find it more alluring than ever. Other times you'll be glad you went away.

The subjects of poetry are always the same, so lend your ear to the language instead. Blaise Pascal said, "Let no one say that I have said nothing new . . . the arrangement of the subject is new. When we play tennis, we both play with the same ball, but one of us places it better."

Dare to say the unsayable in a new way. Ultimately, if a poem does not risk sentimentality, then the poet is not in touch with who he is in the world, not in touch with emotion. And if the poem does not risk absurdity, then the poet isn't even in the game.

THE TELLING THAT SHOWS

Some Provocations from Inside the Story

PETER ROCK

NOT LONG AGO, I was fortunate to hear the excellent Aimee Bender present a talk on that most storied of workshop clichés, "Show, don't tell." One of Aimee's sharp assertions was that telling that succeeds depends on expertise. She asked us to write down five areas in which we felt we possessed some expertise and then had us write a statement or two about these areas. I remember that one woman claimed to be an expert in "interrupting people"; her sentence was "Don't let a person get started or finish a sentence before you leap in." My notes looked like this:

GRILLING STEAK

BARBED WIRE Tightening one strand loosens the others. A corner brace must be a right angle.

SWIMMING

~~NAR~~ BIGFOOT

FISHING IN CANOES Don't paddle as hard when you're

moving with the waves. Paddle harder when you're moving through the shallows.

The five areas in which I claim expertise are clear (though I seem to suggest a near expertise before crossing it out; I wish I could remember what I was thinking), as are the assertions that follow. But as I reflected upon them, I self-consciously began to consider my choices. What kind of person, what character would have these skills, or would claim to have them? An impressive one, a manly one, no doubt. And so I began to think that this list truly demonstrates something about a character. This made me suspect that what I'd been doing in my writing, in pursuit of successful "telling," was also a kind of "showing."

I began to wonder: Is good telling also showing? Is there any successful telling that isn't also showing? And why is bad telling bad, anyway?

In my darker moments as a teacher of creative writing, I wonder if this cliché, "Show, don't tell," is simply unavoidable. Cloaking it under many disguises, I repeat it again and again. Why is this? How can it be avoided? Is there a more productive way to approach this dilemma?

First, let me tentatively define our terms. *Telling* is narration. It can involve exposition, commentary, reflection, hypothesis, and more. *Showing* is action and dialogue, what we often refer to as "scene." One way to think about telling is to compare it to how voice-over works in film (consider for a moment how irritating this can be). A more visual way to understand it is to look at comics: often there is a scene—characters acting, speaking to each other—and then there is a telling set apart at the top or the bottom of the frame, an authoritative voice establishing or commenting upon the narrative, speaking to us from a slightly different time and place.

The telling is the voice of the story; the showing is the characters let loose.

Often there's a disjunction, or a tension, between what is told and what is shown. In fact, nothing feels falser and more contrived than characters who speak and act in perfect alignment with the narration around them. The narrator wants to explain things, to simplify and define them, to have them make sense, but the world won't always be simplified, and people rarely agree on what is happening within it. We recognize such disagreement from our everyday lives, so encountering it in fiction is convincing and believable to us. Here's an example from Denis Johnson's story "Emergency":

I'd never before come across this cemetery. On the farther side of the field, just beyond the curtains of snow, the sky was torn away and the angels were descending out of a brilliant blue summer, their huge faces streaked with light and full of pity. The sight of them cut through my heart and down the knuckles of my spine, and if there had been anything in my bowels I would have messed my pants from fear.

Georgie opened his arms and cried out, "It's the drive-in, man!"

"The drive-in . . ." I wasn't sure what these words meant.

"They're showing movies in a fucking blizzard!" Georgie screamed.

"I see. I thought it was something else," I said.

Throughout the history of literature, there's a great profusion of stories told by child narrators, and crazy narrators, and obsessed narrators, narrators in love, narrators on drugs. One reason such stories often succeed is because the range and focus of their narration are naturally limited, just as their narrators' range of attention and insight is limited. Whatever concerns the narrator, concerns the story. If the story strays from the character, it fails. All first-person narrators *show* as they *tell*, disporting themselves—their obsessions, their blindnesses, their misapprehensions, their insecurities. And, as individual readers who also possess such limitation, such single consciousness, this makes sense to us. The limited, unreliable narrator is often, paradoxically, the one we trust.

Again, a first-person narrator shows as he tells; his mind and concerns shape the story and reveal himself in the process. (To those of you writing nonfiction, this is apparent.) I use the example of "Emergency" because it's an extreme one in which we can see this disportment and disjunction clearly. I would argue, however, that much third-person narration—limited to one character's point of view at a time, following this character's concerns—operates in a similar fashion. Furthermore, I would claim that the telling within stories that possess more removed narrators also shows; these stories reveal their narration's sensibility by the things that are avoided, that go unsaid, and through their focus and structure.

I would even go so far as to say that "omniscient" narrators betray a kind of showing in their focus and their tone, in their slant, in the tension between their telling and the play of the characters. For instance, I remember quite vividly my high school English teacher reading the first line of Jane Austen's *Pride and Prejudice*: "It is a truth universally acknowledged, that a single man in possession of a good fortune, must be in want of a wife."

"Is this 'universally acknowledged'?" Mr. Miller asked us, and my seventeen-year-old self felt a twinge of delight, a sense that for all its bluster and tone, this was a story that was going to allow me to discover its contradictions and prejudices.

Telling closes the distance between the story and the reader; to me, this means that the story speaks—it tells itself, attempting to make sense of itself—and things can become intimate. Whether the narration speaks to us implicitly or explicitly, it is the means through which focus, or limitation, occurs, an interpretation of the action that we can compare to our own.

Showing does not attend to the reader in quite the same way. The characters aren't worried about us; they have enough to worry about. In scene, where things are shown, there is more space for interpretation. The action and dialogue must draw us inside, seduce us, so that we believe in the people involved, so that we care about them and can hurt with them, and especially so that we can understand how to read the tone and slant of the narration around them.

I MUST DIGRESS, for a moment, as I attempt to align the experience of the reader with that of the writer. The following quotation, which I first read in college, has been a continual provocation to me. It's from an essay by Julio Cortázar called "On the Short Story and Its Environs," in his excellent book *Around the Day in Eighty Worlds*:

Horacio Quiroga once attempted a "Ten Commandments for the Perfect Story Teller," whose mere title is a wink at the reader. If none of his commandments may easily be dispensed with, the tenth seems to me perfectly lucid: "Tell the story as if it were only of interest to the small circle of your characters, of which you may be one. There is no other way to put life into the story."

Moments ago I discussed the experience of reading, of coming to believe in the inside of a story. Now I ask you to consider *writing* from the inside, to convince yourself of your characters' dimensions before you attempt to narrate around them or explain them. We always misstep when we consider our writing of a story as a separate action from the story itself; it may also be a mistake to (consciously) consider ourselves at all. Characters would find the suggestion that they are in a story ridiculous and insulting; when writing is truly working, both writer and reader would share this sense of insult, and resent the interruption.

This reminds me of an answer Raymond Carver once gave to an interviewer who asked how much he considered readers' reactions while he was writing: "I'm much more interested in my characters," he said, "in the people in my stories, than I am in any potential reader."

So far I've argued that successful telling shows, or complicates rather than simplifies. I'd like to consider telling that is actually *telling*, and what kind of facts should be told. Let me put it bluntly: shifts in time and space are very rarely occasions for drama and very often occasions for much confusion. It is here that beginning writers often try to write "creatively," to wax and

wane about the tides and the moon or astrology, to discuss horizons or altitudes or Mercator projections. The result is that the
reader stumbles around for several paragraphs before figuring
out where he is. In our early writing, we often have a real aver-
sion to seeming clumsy, or being too straightforward, when the
rule of thumb here should be "If you *can* tell it, tell it."

A good example is the work of Alice Munro, a writer whose
ability to move a story around in time—while maintaining immense clarity and generating startling resonance between
temporal frames—is unparalleled. I decided to investigate her
transitions; paging through her *Selected Stories*, just looking for
line breaks, I came up with these:

> "It was the week before the Labor Day weekend."
>
> "Years later, many years later on a Sunday morning, Rose
> turned on the radio."
>
> "A year or so later Rose was out on the deck . . ."
>
> "The two weeks before Christmas was a frantic time at the
> Turkey Barn."
>
> "I have a picture of the Turkey Barn crew taken on Christmas
> Eve."
>
> "Eva and Ruth are decorating the dinner table on the
> veranda."
>
> "Over cold apple-and-watercress soup Eva has switched
> back . . ."
>
> "By dessert the conversation has shifted to architecture."

Holidays, meals, increments of time: these are not "creative"
transitions. Rather, Munro recognizes that the drama is not in

finding out where we are in time and space, but rather in what happens within moments, and how these moments resonate among themselves. Here, telling is essential; trying to be too subtle with transitions only sows confusion, and this pulls the reader out of the story, perhaps for good.

Along these lines is a great metaphor offered by the film editor Walter Murch, in a footnote within his book *In the Blink of an Eye*:

> A beehive can apparently be moved two inches each night without disorienting the bees the next morning. Surprisingly, if it is moved two *miles*, the bees also have no problem: They are forced by the total displacement of their environment to re-orient their sense of direction, which they can do easily enough. But if the hive is moved two *yards*, the bees will become fatally confused. The environment does not seem different to them, so they do not re-orient themselves, and as a result, they will not recognize their own hive when they return from foraging, hovering instead in the empty space where the hive used to be, while the hive itself sits just two yards away.

To understand what I'm trying to get at, just replace the word *bee* with *reader* and the word *beehive* with *story*.

IF YOU ARE WILLING TO entertain this notion that when writing you should "tell what you know," the question becomes what can we not tell, what must we show, what cannot be simplified? Emotions, for instance. Relationships. And the only way to express such complication is through interaction—often between the characters but sometimes (as I've argued) between the narration and the doings of these characters.

We must know as much about these people as we can. We must believe in them and enter their world before we try to tell their story. In the same way as a reader must directly apprehend and interact with the characters in order to understand how to approach the narration, I believe that writers must first think and write in scene before we narrate, to figure out how to approach our narration. *Who are these people?* We must familiarize ourselves with the inside of the story, so we can write from within it.

Bad telling happens when we betray our anxiety about not knowing enough, when we stand outside the story and try to control it, when we simplify and, in so doing, condescend to our readers and, worse, to our characters. We worry when we ourselves don't believe, so we scramble to explain, we cast nervous asides, we become "Authors."

The story speaks to us. Our relationship, whether writing or reading, is not with the author. I don't mind being interrupted or even frustrated by a narrator, but I cannot abide being reminded of an author. In fact, I've found it helpful to try to avoid thinking of myself as an author or even a writer, but rather to consider myself as a space or consciousness through which narrators and narrations pass.

THOSE MOMENTS IN writing classes when "Show, don't tell" is invoked, however disguised, point to the places where the narration has gone awry, where our authorial anxiety has forced us to try to take control from outside the story, to limit the free will of our characters and our readers so they will understand things as we intend them to, or, equally evil, to impress them with how wise or funny or dexterous we are.

One danger zone is dialogue, which is unsurprising—after all, dialogue gives characters voices, and their voices and their agendas are often different than the narration's. At the moment of ultimate showing, we writers get nervous. We end conversations abruptly. We paraphrase. We allow the characters to tell us about the story, to soliloquize, to have insights into their lives that no real person could manage. We also work very hard to control the part of dialogue that is not in the character's voice—the tags. We have the characters chortle and wheeze and whisper and whine; we use adverbs to remind the reader and reassure ourselves how things are being said. A nice contrast to this tendency is the following conversation, from Ernest Hemingway's story "The Sea Change":

> "No, thanks," he said.
> "It doesn't do any good to say I'm sorry."
> "No."
> "Nor to tell you how it is?"
> "I'd rather not hear."
> "I love you very much."
> "Yes, this proves it."
> "I'm sorry," she said, "if you don't understand."
> "I understand. That's the trouble. I understand."

How mysterious is this situation, how tantalizing! These folks are into some deep drama, and they know what they're talking about. Do we? Not yet, maybe, but we want to. This is because we believe in the characters, and especially because they don't seem eager to explain themselves to us. How different our experience would be if the storytelling were more anxious:

> "No thanks," he said bitterly, the words sharp in his mouth.
> "It doesn't do any good to say I'm sorry?" she poignantly wondered.
> "No." Phil touched her hand with his, then drew it away. He ground his teeth.
> "Nor to tell you how it is?" she Sapphically queried.
> "I'd rather not hear," he groused.
> "I love you very much," she said, perhaps ingenuously.

A lack of confidence exposes the author's hand. To write this way is also to acknowledge the separation between the author's world and that of the characters,' a disjunction that is passed on to the reader.

Recall Hemingway, not actually a confident man, writing in *A Moveable Feast*:

> Since I had started to break down all my writing and get rid of all facility and try to make instead of describe, writing had been wonderful to do.

Another place, paradoxically, where storytelling often goes outside/in is around figural language. All words may be metaphors —coins worn smooth, as one German philosopher would have it; in storytelling, though, we often turn to consciously constructed metaphors.[1] We do this in an attempt to bring greater precision to our description, to bring the reader further and more specifically into our story. We attempt to defamiliarize, to show something in a new way. Metaphors can generate an understanding that is specific to a moment in a story, but they are also dangerous, as they are places where we, when writing, can step outside the story in an effort to impress ourselves or others, or to control and limit a reader's interpretation.

Teaching at a writing conference, I was delighted when a student in a workshop upbraided another: "A writer is only allowed one metaphor a page. That's the rule." While there is no such rule, the notion of one speaks to the real danger: a bad metaphor reminds us of a story's written-ness. Metaphors work best when they remain attuned to and aware of the atmosphere generated by the characters, when they are grounded in the story. A related consideration is simply remaining grounded in the physical. A metaphor that compares an abstraction to another abstraction leaves us grasping at air, while a metaphor that compares one physical act to another can be quite transformative.

For instance, my yoga teacher once instructed me to exhale all my breath and then to wait, wait, until my breath came naturally, when it had to come. He asked me to envision my breath as a small animal, emerging from the burrow of my body. Try this sometime.

Metaphors that compare the physical to the abstract or the metaphysical can also maintain the story's integrity and bring it greater specificity. Here's an amazing example, from Flannery O'Connor's "Parker's Back," that shows an emotional moment, an unconscious turning point, wonderfully visualized:

Until he saw the man at the fair, it did not enter his head that there was anything out of the ordinary about the fact that he existed. Even then it did not enter his head, but a peculiar unease settled in him. It was as if a blind boy had been turned so gently in a different direction that he did not know his destination had been changed.

I VERY RARELY understand talking about writing or writing about writing as discourses that intersect with writing itself. I don't believe that wisdom can be dispensed to writers in this way. How lovely if it were so, and how boring. Instead, I'm always hoping to provoke, to let writers weigh my assertions or learn from my mistakes. May these few thoughts raise questions or disbelief in you.

An exhortation: Convince yourself. Live the delusion. Trust yourself and the people in your stories. Know enough about them to follow them, show them enough sympathy and respect so that they might follow you.

Friend, let me tell you this: telling in stories often attempts to simplify, to clarify, but when it's really working, telling complicates and adds dimension to the experience of the story. It interprets situations and characters, and it invites us to do the same. It involves us.

While I claim expertise in steak grilling and barbed-wire fencing, I have no doubt that there are those who would disagree with my assertions in these areas. Still, I speak from my experience, and I am happy to dispute. I believe in this story I am living; I write to you from within it.

NOTES

1. There is some more experimental writing (I recommend Gary Lutz, Ben Marcus, the unbelievable Diane Williams) in which telling is, explicitly, a kind of showing, a demonstration of how smooth and slippery and broken language is, and words are torn from their familiar contexts, becoming metaphors . . . but here I am talking about more realistic, conventional storytelling, for which the show/tell divide is more easily identified.

GENERATING FICTION FROM
HISTORY AND/OR FACT

JIM SHEPARD

BECAUSE I HAVE the inner emotional life of a ten-year-old, I've always been interested in what one reviewer has called "persistently unusual subjects," and I try, in my own stunted way, to do everything I can while writing to stay in touch with pleasure, with fun, with play, with the passionate engagement that we all experience as children. As Walter Murch, the great Hollywood editor responsible for such films as *Apocalypse Now* and *The Conversation* once pointed out, "As I've gone through life, I've found that your chances for happiness are increased if you wind up doing something that is a reflection of what you loved most when you were somewhere between nine and eleven years old." I've written about Aeschylus at Marathon, the executioner in charge of the Reign of Terror during the French Revolution, Nazi explorers on the hunt for the yeti, high school football players in Texas, reactor engineers during the catastrophe at Chernobyl, and the first female cosmonaut in the Soviet space program. I've recently begun what my agent and I call "the libel cycle," a series

of stories with real figures as their narrator/protagonist: John
Entwistle of The Who; a Yugoslavian soccer star transplanted
to Holland in the 1960s; William Beebe, the inventor of the
bathysphere; John Ashcroft; etc. My father, who is always fear-
fully on the lookout for litigation, once asked me, "Why are
you *doing* this?"

I tell my students that one reason fiction writers are attracted
to nonfiction and/or historical material is that it's a way of enlarging our contact with the world. It's also a way of enlarging
the arena of our autobiographical obsessions. We've all been
told to write what we know, but often, what we know is not
enough, and drawing upon nonfiction and historical material is
a way to expand what we might call "the ground," that element
in our work that prescribes all our choices. When I do it, I'm
looking to complicate my experience and to further interrogate
the relationship between my imagination and my memory. I'm
looking to expand the categorical narrowness of my intellectual
discipline. In other words, I'm recognizing the importance of letting the world teach me. You might liken it to a road trip: you hit
the road and hope that a whole nexus of experience will unspool
before you, that it won't just turn into *I saw a lot of tollbooths.*
When the French novelist Émile Zola wanted to understand
the lives of coal miners in 1884, he descended into the mines to
research what would become his novel *Germinal.* One hundred
and fifty feet below ground he viewed an enormous workhorse
pulling a sled through a tunnel. He asked the miners how they
got the animal in and out of the mine each day. At first they
thought he was joking. When they realized he wasn't, one of

them said, "Mr. Zola, don't you understand? That horse comes down here once, when he's barely more than a foal and can fit in the buckets that bring us down here. He grows up down here. He grows blind down here from lack of light. He hauls coal down here until he can't haul anymore. He dies down here and his bones are buried down here."

That's a metaphor for—and an empathetic understanding of—the miners' lives that the world *taught* Zola and that he had to be receptive to in order to write a book as great as the one he then wrote.

"Well, Jim," you might say, a little peevishly, "that's great for Zola, but what about me?" As a writer, the first issue you have when dealing with historical events has to do with authority, as in "Where do I get off writing about that?" Well, here's some good and some bad news: Where do you get off writing about anything? Where do you get off writing about someone of a different gender? Of a different race? Where do you get off writing about something that never happened to you? Writers shouldn't lose sight of the essential chutzpah involved in trying to imagine another sensibility, and they should take heart in that chutzpah.

The whole project of literature is about the exercise of the empathetic imagination. Why were we given something as amazing as imagination if we're not going to use it? Write what you know? As soon as you start writing, you realize you don't know what you thought you knew. You have to apply your imagination even to your most cherished memories. Remember, as we've been told many times before, we're writing from, but not necessarily about, our lives. Seamus Heaney puts it this way: "I do not suggest that the self is not the proper arena of poetry. But I believe that the greatest work occurs when a certain self-forgetfulness is attained."

SO WHAT HAPPENS when you attempt to write serious fiction about historical situations or real people? Well, the good news is that you're already provided with characters and a situation. The bad news is that those also operate as enormous constraints. Literature that deals with history the most effectively, in my mind, whether it's Marguerite Yourcenar's *Memoirs of Hadrian* or Ron Hanson's "Wickedness" or any number of other novels or stories, understands two things: (A) that fiction about real events needs to respect the facts and (B), as our politicians have taught us, facts are malleable things. The trick, it seems, is to do everything possible to honor A, as you understand it, while taking full advantage of B to shape your material into something aesthetically beautiful. For that reason, I've always found it liberating to write about historical figures about whom there's a lot of mystery. For instance: John Entwistle is the most recessive and mysterious member of The Who. There are a number of books about the other Who members, like Keith Moon, including a biography three inches thick in which he's frequently quoted as saying things like "John Entwistle wasn't around." That gives me room to maneuver. I wrote a novel about F. W. Murnau, a German filmmaker who in biographical terms is one of the more mysterious figures in all of filmmaking. That gave me room to maneuver. Would I want to write a novel about Winston Churchill? I'm not sure. Every moment in the man's life has been interrogated. Every move has been marked down somewhere. In a case like that, I *don't* have much room to maneuver.

A long time ago I read an interview with Allan Gurganus in which he said, "It is the writer's job to take the world personally." I think that's true. The writers I admire take the world personally. It isn't true that only people who live in South LA can write about South LA: people who care enough to learn about South LA can write about South LA. If you can convince me of the reality of something, you have gained an authority.

When I read about The Who, or I read about John Ashcroft, I'm trying to read in a way that energizes not only my imagination but also my emotions. When I'm engaged in what I'm reading in that way, I find myself starting to construct a combination of what I intuit about a subject and what I project upon it. If I don't find something odd and plangent about that subject, then I can't, and don't, write about it.

To cite just one forlorn example: I spent a huge amount of time researching Charles Lindbergh. He was an extraordinarily interesting guy who led an extraordinarily interesting life. Nothing I discovered about him made me think, *This isn't a great story*. But after all that time, I didn't engage with the subject enough to allow me to write the story.

In other words, it isn't the *subject*, in the larger sense, that's the key; it's the more intimate emotional overlaps. I've always been fascinated by German expressionist film. I've read a tremendous amount about all of those filmmakers, but it was Murnau who really resonated with me. It was Murnau whose story I decided to tell.

When a story based on real people is successful, the characters turn into personae—figures that both are and are not those public figures. John Ashcroft is clearly identifiable in my story "John Ashcroft: More Important Things Than Me." He would recognize a lot of his language and a lot of his values. If he were here, he would point and say, *These are the places that it is not me. And this is wrong, by the way. You shouldn't have done this and this.* And then I'd say, *Ha ha ha, I'm writing fiction.* And he'd say, *Ha ha ha, I have a much more powerful lawyer.*

I think that what happens when it works is that I've stumbled onto a shared emotional genealogy with the character that I'm writing about. And that genealogy is what the research helped me more fully uncover. A shared emotional genealogy—or maybe the notion that you can find or create such a thing—makes sense given the project of literature, because as others have pointed out, when we write, we send ourselves as far into another as we can, and then we come back with a sensation that both is and is not our own, but is more complicated. And here's the happy paradox: such distancing seems to enable a new and often much deeper version of emotional honesty and intimacy to be generated, which is crucial to producing original and important work.

As Oscar Wilde put it: "Man is least himself when he talks in his own personae. Give him a mask, and he will tell you the truth." (Now *there's* a weird poster boy for emotional honesty: Oscar Wilde.) The quote of John Ruskin's that serves as a kind of belated epigraph for Marta Morazzoni's novel *The Invention of Truth*—it appears at the end of the book—and from which her title derives, is "We can imagine falsities, we can compose falsehoods, but only the truth can be invented."

For another example of how that kind of aesthetic transformation can operate, consider some excerpts from Nathan
Englander's "The Tumblers," a story that's about a series of
transformations, some of which are historically accurate, some
of which were invented by Englander based on his research.
In the story, a group of strict Jews called the Mahmir Hasidim
from the ghetto of Chelm accidentally board a train of circus
performers while another group—the more relaxed Students of
Mekyl—board a train bound for a concentration camp. This mistake spares the Mahmirim—at least for the moment—and in
this way Englander transforms foolishness into wisdom.

Ironically, it's their strictness that saves the Mahmirim, by
ensuring that they've actually chosen a much better way of surviving in this absurd world:

> Off went the Mekyls to gather bedsteads and bureaus, ham-
> mocks and lawn chairs—all that a family might need in reloca-
> tion. The rabbi of the Mahmir Hasidim, in his infinite strictness
> (and in response to the shameful indulgence of the Mekyls),
> understood "essential" to exclude anything other than one's
> long underwear, for all else was excess adornment.
>
> "Even our ritual fringes?" asked Feitel, astonished.
>
> "Even the hair of one's beard," said the Rebbe, considering
> the grave nature of their predicament.

So Englander arranges it so that they're granted a kind of wisdom by chance. The undeniable murderousness of that moment in
history hasn't been upended by any means—what makes the story's comedy so dark is its insistence that we never lose sight of how

lethal a world it's describing—it's just been a little subverted, and only for the time being. The Mahmirim survive—miraculously, and for the time being—but that miraculousness only highlights how unlikely survival is going to continue to be.

The story goes on to enact exactly what the Germans are enacting, but it also enacts it in such a way that we know something, in spiritual and/or metaphoric terms, is being pushed a little bit. You're not exactly thinking, *That can't be true*, but you're also not thinking *I'll bet that's exactly how it was, how Jews were saved*. The reader is teased with the fact that this is right on the edge of believability and thereby reminded of how much of what the Nazis attempted and accomplished was itself even more outlandishly unbelievable. It's unbelievable that nobody notices that the Mahmirim do not belong on the circus train, but by that point you're invested enough in these people that the idea that their safety depends on an incredibly threadbare disguise is fraught, and not just annoying—I think.

They're magically saved, for now. But elsewhere in the story and with increasing frequency, magical transformation gets freighted with something much darker: historical fact. Even as the story performs its unlikely comic sleight of hand of saving the most improbable of all saved groups, it's reminding us that an entire race is being transformed to extinction:

> Before the dog could reach her and tear her clothes from her skin and the skin from her bones, the sniper on the train put a single bullet through her neck. The bullet left a ruby hole that resembled a charm an immodest girl might wear. Yocheved

touched a finger to her throat and turned her gaze toward the sky, wondering from where such a strange gift had come.

This is death as a kind of mercy—a bullet hole as a ruby— because that train is taking Jews to an extermination camp. The passage is rendered memorable not only through the girl's shock and disbelief but also through the reader's recognition that she is being transformed in a merciful way.

And in that same way, selfishness can be transformed into selflessness, either by fate—if you want to call it that—or by authorial intervention. Mendel, the quasi-protagonist of the story, resolves that he needs a drink so badly that he decides to hell with his compatriots:

> Dismissing the peril to which he was exposing the others, Mendel sought out a benefactor who might sport him a drink. It was in this way—in which only God can turn a selfish act into a miracle—that Mendel initially saved all of their lives.

Mendel, while cadging his drink, chats up one of the circus performers and learns what the Mahmirim will need to do in order to disguise themselves: they need to become clowns. And so Mendel arranges it. And miracle of miracles—it works, at least for the time being, as well:

> Yes, it would be good to have a new group of wiseacres. And they turned in their seats, laughing out loud at these shaved-headed fools, these clowns without make up—no, not clowns, acrobats.

During their chat, the performer also informs Mendel about what's going on in Europe at that point—about the greatest transformation of all:

"Anyway, Günter came to us directly from a performance for the highest of the high where his beautiful assistant Leine had been told in the powder room by the wife of an official of unmatched feats of magic being performed with the trains. They go away full—packed so tightly that babies are stuffed in over the heads of the passengers when there's no room for another full grown—and come back empty, as if never before used."

"And the Jews," asked Mendel. "What trick is performed with the Jews?"

"Sleight of hand," she said, splashing the table with her drink and waving her fingers by way of demonstration. "A classic illusion. First they are here, and then they are gone."

Literature, Englander reminds us, can do the same.

The story transforms victims into survivors. It turns a group of starved, weak Jews into acrobats. It turns, finally, the degraded and the desperate into the exalted and the dignified. That's what art can do. With increasing wonder and anxiety the reader of the story asks, *How are these people going to get away with this? And for how long? Why do I continue to allow myself to hope?* We're hoping time will slow down, but also that it will speed up: we want very much to see if things will go badly, and how badly they'll go. The train arrives at its destination and the Mahmirim prepare to go onstage. Englander grants them their one moment before things start to go awry:

"Hup," cried the Rebbe, and the routine commenced. Shraga cartwheeled and flipped. The widow Raizel jumped once and then stood off to the side with her double-jointed arms turned inside out. Mendel, glorious Mendel, actually executed a springing Half-Hanlon and, with Schmuel Berel's assistance (his only real task), ended in a Soaring Angel.

Then Feitel misses his wife as she leaps toward him and she cracks an ankle, yet she holds her position. Why? Because Englander wants to get them to this point:

Then from above, from off to the left, a voice was heard. Mendel knew from which box it came. He knew it was the most polished, the most straight and tall, a maker of magic, to be sure. Of course, this is conjecture, for how could he see?

"Look," said the voice. "They are as clumsy as Jews." [And the reader is left to decide whether that's the voice of Hitler, or Goering, or God, or whomever, but what we *do* know is that some invisible judge is telling them to perform more, that he loves the farce.] . . .

"More," called the voice. "This farce can't have already come to its end. More!" it said. Another voice, that of a woman, came from the same place and barely carried to the stage.

"Yes, keep on," it said. "More of the Jewish ballet."

And look what happens:

The Rebbe took a deep breath and began to tap with his foot. Mendel waved him off and stepped forward, moving down-

251

stage, the spotlight harsh and unforgiving against his skin. He reached out past the footlights into the dark, his hands cracked and bloodless, gnarled and intrusive.

Mendel turned his palms upward, benighted.

That is a gorgeous and moving image. It's Mendel both as a supplicant to people who will never accept any claim of pity or mercy—but he's stubbornly going to ask for it anyway—and as a goad to their conscience. Imagine doing that as a Jew in an auditorium filled with Nazis. It's a version of "I throw myself on your mercy," but more fully, it's a version of "I throw myself on your mercy knowing full well there will be no mercy. But someday you will think of this moment. You will think about the moment that we stopped playing for you, and we said, *You are going to kill us.* And you will remember the way we held on to our dignity and the way we held your humanity to account."

You can *feel* that emotion, and yet Englander wasn't there. This is quite far from direct history, and yet it's based on real history.

So here's what I'm trying to assert: that the song of everyone else that we seem to be composing when we write about others slowly evolves into a song of ourselves. People who are suspicious of such methods, and who only allow themselves to be moved by stories that are directly autobiographical in their events, as if all literature aspires to the condition of the memoir, mistakenly equate a plain style, or what seems to be an unmediated or autobiographical set of events, with sincerity. Which is a little bit like saying vanilla ice cream is more sincere than chocolate chip.

I think it was Gurganus who said that one of the main reasons we write literature is because there's probably nothing more profound than imagining other people's lives, and nothing less profound. The favor of doing that might be the best thing we can do for each other. We have to give ourselves over to other people, no matter how intimidating or frustrating that process might be.

I think of it as the most useful sort of human exchange. In turning over my imagination to these distant and initially strange sensibilities, I'm continually giving myself away—in both senses of the phrase—and I'm continually gathering others into me, in a way that Walt Whitman wrote about much more eloquently, but in a way that I hope he would recognize.

CONTRIBUTORS

DOROTHY ALLISON was born in Greenville, South Carolina, but makes her home in Northern California, with her partner, Alix, and her teenage son, Wolf Michael. She is the author of *Bastard out of Carolina, Trash, Two or Three Things I Know for Sure*, and more. She writes out of a deep unexplainable need to try and be at home in the world. But she's not, she's just not.

STEVE ALMOND is the author of five books, most recently *Not That You Asked*, an essay collection. He lives outside Boston with his wife and kids.

RICK BASS is the author of twenty-four books of fiction and nonfiction, including, most recently, *The Wild Marsh*. He lives in western Montana, where he has long been active in efforts to protect as wilderness the last roadless lands of the Yaak Valley.

SUSAN BELL is the author of *The Artful Edit: On the Practice of Editing Yourself* (W.W. Norton & Co., 2007) and coauthor with Jason West of *Dare to Hope: Saving American Democracy*, a collection of essays on political activism (Miramax, 2005). She has written for several publications, including *Tin House,* the *London Sunday Telegraph,* and *Vogue,* and for National Public Radio's program *Berlin Stories.* A former editor at Random House and *Conjunctions* magazine, Bell teaches at the New School's graduate writing program in New York City and at the Tin House Summer Writers Workshop.

AIMEE BENDER is the author of three books—*The Girl in the Flammable Skirt, An Invisible Sign of My Own,* and *Willful Creatures.* Her short fiction has been published in *Granta, GQ, Harper's,* the *Paris Review, Tin House, McSweeney's,* and more and has received two Pushcart Prizes. She is currently at work on a novel and regularly teaches at the Tin House Summer Writers Workshop in July.

KATE BERNHEIMER is the author of two novels, *The Complete Tales of Merry Gold* (FC2, 2006) and *The Complete Tales of Ketzia Gold* (FC2, 2002). She has edited two essay collections, *Mirror, Mirror on the Wall: Women Writers Explore Their Favorite Fairy Tales* (Anchor/Vintage, 2002) and *Brothers and Beasts: An Anthology of Men on Fairy Tales* (Wayne State University Press, 2007). She is also the author of two children's books, *The Girl in the Castle Inside the Museum* (Random House, 2008) and *The Lonely Book* (forthcoming, Random House). Founder and editor of the journal *Fairy Tale Review,* her stories and essays have appeared in, among other places, *Western Humanities Review,* the *Massachusetts Review, Tin House,* and *Marvels & Tales: The Journal of Fairytale Studies.*

LUCY CORIN is the author of the short story collection *The Entire Predicament* (Tin House Books, 2007) and the novel *Everyday Psychokillers: A History for Girls* (FC2, 2004). Recent stories appear in *Conjunctions* and the *Massachusetts Review*. She has been a fellow at both Bread Loaf and the Sewanee Writers' Conference, and she's associate professor in the English department at the University of California, Davis.

TOM GRIMES is the author of the novels *WILL@epicqwest. com*, *A Stone of the Heart*, *Season's End*, *Redemption Song*, and *City of God*. He edited the fiction anthology *The Workshop: Seven Decades of Fiction from the Iowa Writers' Workshop*. His essay "Bring Out Your Dead" appeared in *Tin House* and was a Notable Essay of 2007. His interview with Roddy Doyle appears in the interview anthology *The World Within*. He directs the MFA Program in Creative Writing at Texas State University.

MATTHEA HARVEY's most recent book of poetry, *Modern Life*, won the Kingsley Tufts Poetry Award and was a New York Times Notable Book of 2008 as well as a finalist for the National Book Critics Circle Award. She is also the author of *Sad Little Breathing Machine* and *Pity the Bathtub Its Forced Embrace of the Human Form* and a forthcoming children's book, *The Little General and the Giant Snowflake*. A contributing editor to *jubilat*, *BOMB*, and *Meatpaper*, she teaches poetry at Sarah Lawrence and lives in Brooklyn.

ANNA KEESEY is a graduate of the Writers' Workshop at the University of Iowa. She is the recipient of a number of prizes and fellowships for her fiction, which has appeared in *Grand Street*, *Doubletake*, *Nimrod*, *Witness*, and other journals, as well as in Houghton-Mifflin's Best American Short Stories series. She has taught creative writing at Northwestern University and Washington University in St. Louis, among other schools. Currently she teaches writing and literature at Linfield College in McMinnville, Oregon.

JIM KRUSOE has published poetry, two books of stories, and two novels, *Iceland* (Dalkey Archive Press) and *Girl Factory* (Tin House Books). His novel *Erased* is scheduled for publication by Tin House in 2009. He lives in Los Angeles.

MARGOT LIVESEY is the author of a collection of stories and six novels, including *Eva Moves the Furniture* and, most recently, *The House on Fortune Street*. She is a distinguished writer in residence at Emerson College.

ANTONYA NELSON is the author of nine books of fiction, including *Nothing Right* (Bloomsbury, 2009). She teaches creative writing at the University of Houston and lives in New Mexico, Colorado, and Texas.

CHRIS OFFUTT is the author of two books of short stories, *Kentucky Straight* and *Out of the Woods*; two memoirs, *The Same River Twice* and *No Heroes*; and a novel, *The Good Brother*. His work has been widely anthologized, translated into eight languages, and taught in high schools and colleges. He has taught creative writing at the Iowa Writers' Workshop, the University of New Mexico, the University of Montana, and Mercer University.

D. A. POWELL's books include *Tea, Lunch, Cocktails* (finalist for the National Book Critics Circle Award) and *Chronic*. His honors include a fellowship from the National Endowment for the Arts and awards from the Academy of American Poets and the Poetry Society of America. Powell teaches in the English department at the University of San Francisco.

PETER ROCK is from Utah. He now lives in Portland, Oregon, with his wife and children. The author of five novels, most recently, *My Abandonment*, and a collection of stories, *The Unsettling*, he teaches writing at Reed College and enjoys drinking cocktails at the expense of Tin House.

JIM SHEPARD is the author of six novels, including most recently *Project X*, and three story collections, including most recently *Like You'd Understand, Anyway*. His short fiction has appeared in, among other magazines, *Harper's*, *McSweeney's*, the *Paris Review*, the *Atlantic Monthly*, *Esquire*, *Granta*, the *New Yorker*, and *Playboy*. He teaches at Williams College.

COPYRIGHT NOTES AND PERMISSIONS

"Place," copyright © 2008 by Dorothy Allison. First delivered as a lecture at the Tin House Summer Writers Workshop.

"Hard Up for a Hard-on," copyright © 2007 by Steve Almond. First delivered as a lecture at the Tin House Summer Writers Workshop.

"When to Keep It Simple," copyright © 2009 by Rick Bass.

"Revisioning *The Great Gatsby*," copyright © 2004 by Susan Bell. First printed in *Tin House* no. 20.

"Character Motivation," copyright © 2006 by Aimee Bender. First delivered as a lecture at the Tin House Summer Writers Workshop.

"Fairy Tale Is Form, Form Is Fairy Tale," copyright © 2009 by Kate Bernheimer.

"Material," copyright © 2009 by Lucy Corin.

"There Will Be No Stories in Heaven," copyright © 2009 by Tom Grimes.

"The Mercurial World of the Mind," copyright © 2004 by Matthea Harvey. First printed in *Crowd* no. 4.2.